Writing and Enjoying Haiku

Writing
and
Enjoying
Haiku

A Hands-on Guide

Jane Reichhold

KODANSHA INTERNATIONAL
Tokyo • New York • London

DEDICATION

blue ink
the words not yet written
in the iris

Distributed in the United States by Kodansha America, LLC, and in the United Kingdom and continental Europe by Kodansha Europe Ltd.

Published by Kodansha International Ltd., 17–14 Otowa 1-chome, Bunkyo-ku, Tokyo 112–8652.

ISBN 978–4–7700–2886–0

First edition, 2002
20 19 18 17 16 15 14 13 12 11 10   12 11 10 9 8 7 6

www.kodansha-intl.com

CONTENTS

FOREWORD
Toward Enjoyment

Though the word "enjoying" is the third word in the title of this book, for me enjoying anything and everything is the primary function of our lives. True, the function of this book is to teach you how to write haiku, but I want you to first learn to touch a point of pleasure within yourself with haiku.

To do this, you will need to open the arms of your mind to take in some haiku already snapped up out of the air and written down.

Because the haiku in the following selection are all connected to one subject, with a wide variety of techniques and levels of complication, you can explore them with a gentle touch of your eyes as if looking over a branch to choose which flowers you might pick. You do not have to like or understand all of them, but just take up each one and examine it carefully.

Read them not only to see what has been thought, and to delight in this sharing, but allow the words to move across any similar memory or past idea you may have had. In this way the haiku pick up your patterns as iron filings arrange themselves on a magnet to be changed in a once-in-a-lifetime relationship.

Even as you do this, it is possible the writer in you will begin itching to change a word here and there. Something small and loud and very close to you will want to put the words in a different way than I have, or even to write a line on a totally dissimilar subject. Listen to these urges and begin here, beside my words, to write your own versions of the poems in the wide spaces on the page (assuming you have not borrowed this book from the local library).

Toss out the memory of the teacher who told you never to mark in your books and tell your inner critic, who might be insisting you know nothing about haiku, just to back off and be quiet. Think only that you have decided to enjoy seeing where these haiku lead you, and to explore what they find within you.

I want this book to be your book—with sentences underlined, comments written in the margins, your poems on the flyleaves, and your first thoughts beside these haiku in the introduction.

Go slowly. Take each haiku separately; read and reread until you have completely thought through it, around it, and beyond it. Write down whatever thoughts come to your mind before moving on to the next haiku, even if you need to get a separate pad of paper. Tape the pages of your words among my words. Do the altered book artthing. Make these pages a symbiotic work between the two of us.

Let go of any preconceived ideas and simply do whatever brings you the most enjoyment. This is your life, the book you are writing.

silence
between words
stories

desert
stretched to the horizon
silence

silence
when naked and alone
a tunnel

pond lilies
floating in their centers
silence

silence
in a rain shower
seven colors

winter leaves
buds of tightly rolled
silence

silence
around a waiting bird
the nest

silence
after the hailstorm
colder

silver-tipped firs
snow deepening
silence

silence
between crashing waves
the briefness of foam

riptide
in the sea the pull of
silence

silence
drawing together lovers
a silver cord

a blossom's dance
the urges deep within
silence

Later, when you have read the rest of this book, do come back here to see yourself as you were in the beginning. I think you'll be surprised how much you already knew, and also how much richer your writing life has become, due to this hands-on guide.

Blessed be,
Jane Reichhold

One

FOUR THINGS TO DO BEFORE WRITING HAIKU

Learn How to Read Haiku

Before you can learn to write haiku, you need to be able
to read haiku. That sounds fairly simple, but like every-
thing else concerned with haiku, levels are buried under
levels and archeology seems child's play in warm sand.
To uncover some of the mysteries of haiku, let us begin
by digging below the surface of this haiku:

> moving into the sun
> the pony takes with him
> some mountain shadow

The first line, if taken literally, sets up an impossibil-
ity—nothing of our earth can truly move into the sun.
However, earthly things can move into an area where the
sun is shining. Already the brevity of haiku demands that
the reader try to find a meaning since the line is a frag-
ment which lacks an object. The reader, wanting to be
able to form a mental image, needs an object, and so
rapidly moves his or her eyes to the second line. Ah, "the
pony takes with him"; there is the answer—the pony—

but already the rest of the line, "takes with him," sets up the desire for more information. The reader is now unable to stop reading the haiku in an eagerness to find out the rest of the story. The answer—"some mountain shadow." Now, what does that mean?

The reader then goes back to the first line. Now it is understood that it is the pony that is moving into the sun, and it is taking with him some of the shadow of the mountain. It is fairly common to speak of the shadow of a mountain and the shadow of a pony, but to see that the shadow of a pony has moved away some of the mountain's shadow for itself is a new way of viewing a natural phenomenon. All of these steps and the further pondering of the meaning of the images is the very active participation of the reader in reading a haiku.

Experienced haiku readers will automatically follow and understand this process and the journey. Sometimes beginning readers need to have additional information to completely understand the haiku. For them, it might help to know about the situation that gave rise to the inspiration for this haiku.

I was sitting at the window of a hotel at a mountain resort watching some ponies grazing early in the morning on a valley meadow that was still partially covered with the shadow of the nearby hillside. As the grazing pony moved slowly into the sunshine, I happened to be focused on the edge of the shadow and actually saw some of the mountain's shadow follow the pony. The line of shadow seemed to break off and reshape itself to become pony shadow.

At a philosophical level, the haiku can also be expressing the idea that when something—like a person—moves into the light, there will still be, not only the slender shadow in person shape, but also a remnant of our greater shadow from which we have come.

It can also be thought that the pony, by eating the grass of the mountain, becomes the mountain in the same way the shadows of these things move between the objects. When the boundaries disappear between separate things, it is truly a holy moment of insight, and it is no wonder that haiku writers are educated to latch on to these miracles and to preserve them in words.

Teachers have been telling students for years that a haiku is a poem about nature written in seventeen syllables. That is plain and simple enough. Perhaps you wrote a haiku in school and had it posted on the bulletin board. And yet, now years later, as the image of the inspiration remains in your mind, you suspect that there is more to haiku than you had thought there was. You are right.

Many people who take up an interest in haiku do so because they are looking for more structure, not only in their writing, but also in their lives. Somehow people always think that times have never been as chaotic as they are today.

Having a set of rules to follow gives purpose to actions, exerts a sense of control over the moment, and builds confidence in the exercise of "I can do this." And there is no form of poetry that comes with more rules and instructions, do's and don'ts than haiku. For some persons this idea is a comfort, and learning the rules is an easy path to quick success. For those of you who are into freedom and complete exercise of your personality, what if you were told you can make up your own rules of writing haiku and change them as often as you want? For both ways, however, you must first learn what rules have been followed in the past before you start making changes.

Maybe you have read a haiku somewhere, and the idea in it was such a surprise and such a delight that you have become intrigued with the form. You may have almost no interest in poetry as such, yet you have been attracted to the intrigue of an unusual perception that came with the haiku that so strangely spoke to you.

Perhaps you were impressed by a haiku translated from the Japanese, and thus it may be hard for you to follow that example to write your own haiku in English. Not all translations are set in good English haiku style. Because of the vast differences in the two languages, and because many early translators were language experts and not poets, you will also find a wide variety of versions of the same Japanese haiku in the second language. Even though you may love best the Japanese haiku, you need to see how English writers are changing and modifying the haiku to fit another language and culture.

When any poetry form makes the transition from one culture to another, it usually becomes revitalized. The old form blends and bends with new ideas, new concepts, and new ways. This is what is happening to the four-hundred-year-old Japanese haiku as it cohabits with other languages and cultures around the world. We are not Japanese, and what we write in English can never be a Japanese haiku. But we have recognized the value of the spirit and the techniques of the Japanese haiku and have been able to incorporate them into our poems. Thus, most of us continue to call our little poems "haiku" to honor the lineage.

Some people come to haiku as a way of capturing the present moment. Just as there are occasions and moments when we wish to take a photograph, there are events and situations that we wish to conserve, contain, and retain. With only our minds and what we have learned, we are able to preserve that thought, or idea or inspiration, with such validity and perfection that any rereading of a haiku will instantly return us to a particular place or situation. Haiku act as doors to our past. Years after you have written a haiku, you can read it and mentally return to that one spot in the meadow where you saw the purple thistle glistening with dew, or heard the long curling cry of a bird on a summer morning.

Haiku focus on the here and now. This forces one to "be in the moment" instead of running the debilitating dialogues which too often project like bad films in our heads. Haiku forces us to get out of the loops of worries or depressing thoughts by demanding that we use our senses to explore what is around the body at this very second. Teachers of meditation speak of "getting in touch with ourselves" as a way of centering. Here is haiku showing you how marvelous this one second of your life is. In the search for haiku we rely on what our senses are telling us, not what we have been taught is true or think we believe is true. Haiku are written from experience, not from knowledge or belief or idea. They are actual, concrete, and securely cemented to the present—whenever it happens.

Know Why You Want to Write Haiku

The first answer is "because you can!" Most of the arts demand training and mastering complicated materials. Haiku can be spoken and left simply to hang in the air. Or you can write them down on the smallest piece of paper—to save and savor the thought of your moment of inspiration. Once you begin to save your thoughts, you will more carefully notice the thoughts of others which have been saved as haiku.

As we evolve away from tribal living and thinking, the individual value of the person intensifies. With increased freedom we are able to develop into more distinct parts of humanity. One way of expressing our distinctness is with words, and that can be with the haiku we write. As our skills with words are honed, as the techniques become second nature, the haiku even more faithfully reflect the individuality of a person. Really all we have to offer the world is the gift of our individuality. We can never be just like any other person. Our journey through life is an extremely personal contribution to the work of being human.

Maybe you have always loved poetry but thought, "I could never write anything like that." But don't you think you could write a haiku? Wouldn't it be great to give it a try? And who knows?

Each of us will have our own personal reason for wanting to write haiku. For me, the way I live in order to be prepared to receive haiku inspiration is more valuable than the poems I finally do write. You see, in order to be open to being given the haiku (and I do believe they are given to us as gifts) we need to go through life with a certain attitude. People actually speak of living The Way of Haiku. This does not mean you must become a Zen Buddhist, or live on a remote mountain wearing a robe, sit with your legs crossed, or try to be anyone but yourself. But there are distinct attitudes that will increase and enrich the haiku you write as well as your life.

1. Being aware—This means just being in the moment, using your senses to test each environment anew all the time, noticing what is around and how each part relates to the other. Instead of thinking thoughts, you use your mind to check out what is. This is also called "centering" because when you can shut down the voice within that nags, complains, and irritates, you reach a state of equilibrium.

> out of earth
> the flower shape
> of a hole

By actually seeing that the hole dug for the seed already has the shape of a flower, one has a new awareness of dirt and flowers and their relationship.

2. Being nonjudgmental—Most of our lives and much of our inner dialogue with ourselves involves saying, "This is good" and "That is bad." This kind of thinking about ourselves feeds and supplies that nagging voice within that is so disruptive to our peace of

mind. The more we can view everything and everyone as being neither good nor bad but as simply being what they are, the easier it is to shut down that inner voice and open ourselves up to the majesty of the world around us.

> a mouse and I share
> her nest in the sock drawer
> a house in the woods

Instead of freaking out over finding a mouse in the drawer, one accepts that living in the woods, where mice live, means that living spaces are going to overlap.

3. Being reverent—To appreciate the smallness that is the grandness of haiku one needs a reverence for life. This means not only a kindly feeling for other persons, and a gentleness with other living beings, but also a sacred handling of the things that we normally do not think as living—rocks, rivers, mountains, houses, rooms, and utensils. When we live as if everything is sacred, which it is if you really think about it, we relate to the things in our environment in a much more responsible way. When one really understands the marvels in a square inch of earth—its history, its journey, its purposes, the vast richness of its being—how can one pollute it, desecrate it, or demean it?

There is a story told of Bashō and his favorite student, Kikaku. One day Kikaku, who was very impulsive and the wit of the group, came running up to Bashō with his newest and most wonderful verse.

Probably dancing and gesturing broadly, Kikaku read:

> pulling off
> the wings of the dragonfly
> a red pepper

You see what his thought was, don't you? In Japan there is a species of large dragonflies with bright red bodies. If you pulled the wings off the curving, pointed body, what remained would look like a small red pepper.

Very quietly, and with a gentle smile, Bashō offered a correction:

> adding wings
> to the red pepper
> a dragonfly

4. Having a sense of oneness—The above example also exhibits the idea that all things are in all things. There *is* a red pepper in the dragonfly. Often the reality of this thinking comes in an experience, known as "satori" or enlightenment, when the person comprehends the completeness, the oneness of all existence. Instead of looking at the world for differences, if we search for the common ground, it becomes easier for us to get along with each other as humans and in the world of nature. Some of the techniques of haiku are built on the idea that even very dissimilar things have a common bond. Finding this fulcrum point is the basis for many, many haiku.

finding connections

starfish
all the days of a life
going into a gull

One aspect that pulls the things of the world together is the food chain. Life, and the passage of the time of a life, is taken from one to be given to another. Even the material of stars is exchanged between us.

5. Having a sense of simplicity—Haiku, as no other poetry form, demands simplicity. Not only are the subjects of haiku the simple things of life, but the way of writing must be simple, with a succinct and exact use of words. In paring down our words, as well as our view of the world, we come to understand that in this age of increasing commercialism, it is beautiful to adopt simple ways, simple things—to have in life only the necessities. To surround ourselves with the beauty of form instead of ornamentation, with the patina of the well-used instead of the shine of the new, with the genuine thing instead of a copy, is a way to profoundly change our inner being.

slender coolness
a finger-wide waterfall
into cupped hands

6. Having humility—The writing of haiku is a practice in humility in many ways. First of all, you will be humbled as you begin to explore the majesty of even the most common things around you. As you learn to

look more deeply into each aspect of the universe, the reason, the intelligence, the glory of it will fill you with awe. Secondly, contemporary poetry is based on what the author feels or thinks—which is extremely ego-inflating. Haiku is based on what the author observes. Thus, the focus is not on the inside world, but on the outside world. Often this is a step that is very hard for some beginners to take—to stop wanting to tell others what they think, feel, believe, or wish to have thought of as reality. For them it is a major advancement to put these goals aside and simply to report on what is. The putting away of personal pronouns in your haiku writing is evidence that this step has been taken.

Another factor of humility that haiku teaches is that you are not the author of any of the haiku. They are gifts given to you by your spirits. They come through you but are not yours. Thus, there is no way the greatness of any of your haiku can add to your estimation of yourself. As soon as you understand that you are already great, wonderful, and magnificent, as you truly are, you are on the way to loving yourself and will not need the adulation of others. If someone likes your haiku, this tells you much about that person and adds nothing to your own value. Because the haiku only come through you, you can be genuinely proud of them. In the same way that you would show someone a marvelous gift that your closest friend has made and given to you, you bring a basket of the most perfect apples from your tree to your neighbor.

Being in this state, or even having a flash of inspiration, will not guarantee that the haiku is good, great, or even a haiku. For that, one must know how to write and, even more specifically, how to write a haiku. There has been a myth passed around the haiku scene that if one has a worthy, deep, or lasting "haiku moment," the resulting poem will be a great haiku. This, as all myths, is partly true and fraudulently false. If one knows how to write haiku, the inspiration may seem to write itself in a haiku by itself. Even if one is only barely acquainted with haiku, this moment may bring the greatest haiku of all. It can also be that the experience is so mind-blowing that one never really finds the single best haiku to convey the feelings. What surely will happen is that the glory of the moment of inspiration will be so fantastic that no matter whether the resulting haiku is seen as good or weak by others, it remains as a touchstone for you and for your special moment.

Since it takes only a little training to become an excellent haiku writer (believe it or not!), there has to be another factor in determining whether your work will appeal or not. In addition to being able to write, and to use words effectively, I believe the author's other most important task is spiritual training. I find that I most easily appreciate the haiku of the most developed souls—the persons who have attained a certain emotional and spiritual maturity.

Be Ready to Change Your Ideas of Poetry

Poetry is what happens between the words. Words are

like signposts or waymarkers that allow the reader to follow the steps the author's mind has taken to come to a poetic idea. Vision is seeing, and in seeing we recognize the thing which is portrayed in a new way.

Sometimes it seems it would be easier to paint pictures because it is the eyes that are used in vision. But pictures are too flat, too one-dimensional. In poetry we do use pictures, but we demand that the reader supply them. I can say "house" and you will see a dwelling. Thanks to our emotional wiring you will not see some unknown house, but most likely one that is very precious to you— your own! Thus, the image comes not only with pictorial information of bricks and boards but also packs emotional baggage.

In prose the writer gently guides the reader attention from one point to another. Poetry is faster, and haiku comes at the reader at warp speeds. Instead of holding your hand and giving you one idea after another in a steady stream, haiku flips you an image and says, "Here, picture this," and you do. In the next line comes the pointer to another image, which you combine with the previous one. This is why haiku and most other poetry have an uneven right-hand margin—so you have a place to put the image which the words to the left have called up in you. Your eyes quickly race from left to right (if you are reading English) along a line of print and then *boom!*

> the words stop
> and the mind smoothly continues
> – the visual picture

From the above, you can see that haiku is not simply the chopping off of a chunk of Western poetry, arranging it into three lines, and making it look like a haiku. Many persons who first begin to write haiku, and in this category are many well-known and well-published poets, think they can retain their normal methods of writing poetry and pass it off as haiku.

Find Out What a Haiku Is

The haiku in Japan and the haiku of the rest of the world are almost two different genres. Though the haiku written in languages not Japanese have various common aspects, the Japanese haiku has a set of parameters not possible in other languages and cultures.

In Japan the haiku is composed of three parts containing five sound units (*on*) in the first section or line, seven sound units in the second part, and five in the final part. There have been a few experiments by Japanese ancestors to change this pattern, but the feeling for the rightness of this is so ingrained in their literary history that, as a folk, they seem unable to give up counting the sound units in their haiku.

The second most important aspect of a Japanese haiku is that it contains a so-called season word—*kigo*, KEY-GO. This is a word or term that indicates the time of the year in which the haiku was written or takes place. These time-honored phrases act as kick starters for the reader's imagination by instantly taking him or her to the proper place in the year to unfold the haiku.

The Japanese recognized the ability of the human

brain to organize information in the manner of an almanac and have capitalized on it in a major way with their own short poetry.

Because Japan is a long, thin north–south country, the indications of the seasons start in the south and move north over a period of several months. To correct for this, all the seasonal references are set to the time the aspects appear in Tokyo, the capital. In some cases this makes the designation somewhat arbitrary as they try to tie events to an actual calendar. It is even more astounding when a thing is placed in a certain season because a famous poem placed it there.

When haiku came to the Western world, there was very little instruction about the importance of season words because at that time no one had yet translated a compendium of seasonal words (*saijiki,* SIGH-GEE-KEY), nor had one been compiled in English. Thus, the imported haiku was stripped of an explanation of this very necessary aspect of Japanese haiku. Our inability to place our haiku in their traditional seasons was another reason Japanese authorities saw a difference between our haiku and theirs. They would try to teach us about season words by holding contests based on a subject, but since we lacked a knowledge of their literary history, we could not keep within the boundaries of the usage in the way they knew from the poems they had grown up with. We tended to mix seasons and subjects to a distressing degree.

Finally, in 2000, one of the largest haiku groups in Japan—the Shiki Salon of Matsuyama University—issued a manifesto decreeing that non-Japanese haiku were not required to contain a *kigo* or season word. Yet it was so hard for them to give up this age-old idea that they suggested we foreigners adopt a system of "keywords." When one thinks of designating certain words into seasonal categories so they mean the same thing to all cultures, all latitudes, and all attitudes, the utilization of this suggestion boggles the mind. Just think of Australians' hot weather in January as a source for topsy-turvy season words. Yet the permission to call our work haiku without the proper use of season words was considered by some to be a big step in the direction of what was already being done. And you thought haiku was easy—and simple!

Two

THE GUIDE TO
HAIKU WRITING

Clearing up the Conflict over Counting Syllables

Many people, when they learn even the most basic information about haiku, are told that haiku should consist of seventeen syllables divided into three lines. You can take up this rule as one for your work if you wish, as a great number of people have done, but the method has several major problems due to differences in our languages that you should carefully consider.

1. What a Japanese person is counting when composing a haiku are called *on*, which at times have been translated as "syllables" but which are now called "sound units." There is a huge difference between English syllables and Japanese sound units. Written in the English alphabet, sound units can be as short as one letter (*a*, *i*, *u*, *e*, *o*, *n*), but they more often consist of two letters, a consonant and a vowel (e.g., *ka*, *ki*, *ku*, *ke*, *ko*). All sound units end in a vowel except for *n*, which is considered a sound unit in its own right; thus *tanka*, which we would consider to have two syllables in English (tan-ka), has three sound units according to the Japanese

way of counting (ta-n-ka). The word *haiku* itself has two syllables in English but three sound units in Japanese (ha-i-ku). Again, the word *Tokyo* can have two or three syllables in English (depending on whether it is pronounced To-kyo or To-ky-o), but in Japanese it has four sound units (To-u-kyo-u). As you can see from this, counting syllables in English and Japanese are quite different procedures. This brings seriously into question the rule that English haiku should be written in 5-7-5 syllables because that is the way it is done in Japanese.

Add to this the differences in vocabulary and syntax, and this rule becomes even more problematic. Take the sentence "He ate an apple," for example, and translate it into Japanese: *Kare wa ringo o tabeta*. The English sentence has five syllables while the Japanese has ten sound units. Even from this simple example one could draw the conclusion that English is able to say in fewer syllables what Japanese take more sound units to express.

In fact, many comparisons have found that an English haiku with seventeen syllables will contain about a third more information than a Japanese haiku. This situation seems acceptable until one tries to translate any of these seventeen-syllable English haiku into Japanese or wishes to write a modern haiku. When reading accurate, not padded-out translations from the Japanese, contemporary writers have seen that the original haiku, put into English translations, look and sound much shorter. Thus, we have adopted the method of using less than seventeen English syllables in our haiku. You cannot have it both ways. You have to decide if you wish for your haiku to equate with the process (counting parts of the poem) or with the product (the more focused, actual information in a haiku).

2. Japanese writers usually do not use punctuation marks as we do, with a dot for a period, but employ words called "cutting words," *kireji*, KEY-RAY-GEE. Thus *ka* and *kana* would be similar to our speaking or writing out "dash" or "comma." These words of punctuation, some as verb or adjective suffixes, are also used as emphasis and carry various emotional messages as well. Often these are translated as "alas!" or "oh!" This is the same as when we use the exclamation point to indicate that the author feels emphatically about something. The employment of cutting words uses up one or two of the sound units, shortening the factual information package of the haiku by up to twelve percent.

3. The Japanese author can pick from a variety of sizes of cutting words in order to make a too-short line fit the counting scheme without adding information. The non-Japanese writer has no help which is similar.

4. The English language, though it has many five- or seven-syllable phrases, has even more that lack a syllable or two. Thus, to make the phrase fit to the syllable count, the author adds extra words—usually unnecessary adjectives and adverbs. In a form where brevity rules, this is a sure way to add a distraction that the haiku does not need.

There have been authorities who have advanced various theories on guidelines we should follow in English that involve counting the beats in the haiku or the stresses, so that we are all using the very same arrangement. If you wish to investigate this method (and if you understand beats in language and how stresses are viewed), you can follow a system of two beats, three beats, two beats.

One goal of all this counting is to use as few words as possible to set the signposts which lead the reader to follow the inspiration of the author. Therefore, it seems counterproductive to follow any setup that encourages the adding of extra words or images just to fill up a preconceived quota.

Another theory suggests that the haiku should not be longer than what a person can speak in one breath. The problem with this guideline is that the haiku has two parts, and it is often the slight intake of breath that separates them. So, yes, the haiku should only be as long as one breath, but it takes two breaths to speak it correctly. The idea, even here, is that the haiku should be as short as possible.

It is interesting to note that, for the most part, haiku in English are set into three lines whereas in Japanese they are generally written in one vertical line. "Why is this?" one could ask. The reason is, to a Japanese it is very clear that the haiku contains three parts, and when they hear a haiku spoken, they immediately recognize the beginning and the ends of the three parts. We have a similar recognition in English. We know "in the garden" is a phrase and "in the" is not a phrase. What English does not have is a history of composing phrases with either five or seven sound units as the Japanese do.

Thus, for us to show these three parts in our language, we have devised the practice of giving each part a typographical line.

Whether you fill the lines of your own haiku with seventeen syllables, or make your lines short, long, short, is a decision which you as a writer will have to make. There are staunch proponents of both methods. Which example below seems to fit your idea of what a haiku should be?

evening settles down
the moor hen on seven eggs
dew upon the grass

or

lightning
a heron's cry stabs
the darkness*

The Fragment and Phrase Theory

The guideline which has been followed the longest, and is by far the most important to the form, asserts that a haiku must be divided into two sections. This is the positive side of the other rule that haiku should not be a run-on sentence, or sound like a complete sentence with each line fitting neatly into the next. There needs to be a syntactical break separating the verse into two distinct divisions. From the Japanese-language examples, this meant

---

* Matsuo Kinsaku, better known as Bashō.

that one line—five sound units—was separated from the rest by either grammar or punctuation.

For the purposes of this discussion, I would like to call the shorter portion "the fragment," and the longer portion, or two-line remainder of the poem, "the phrase."

The need for distinguishing between the two sections of the haiku takes on importance when one begins to discuss the use of articles—a, an, & the—because it is possible to have different rules for these two parts. Before getting into that, let me state that the fragment can be, or usually is, either in the first line or in the last one—either of the short lines. Here is an example for you to test your ability to distinguish the two parts of a haiku.

> rain gusts
> the electricity goes
> on and off

Even without punctuation the reader can hear and feel the break between the fragment, "rain gusts," and the phrase, "the electricity goes on and off." The second line break could occur after "goes," yet, another author may find merit in continuing the line to read "the electricity goes on," and then let the final line bring in the dropped shoe—"and off." Here the goal was to establish an association between "rain gusts" and the way they go "on and off." One can write of many qualities of "rain gusts," but in this verse the "on and off" aspect is brought forward and then reinforced by bringing in the intermittent flickering of the electric lights.

An example of placing the fragment in the third line is in the next haiku.

the cemetery fence
is unable to hold back
white lilies

If the fragment in the last line was written as "the white lilies," the haiku would have been a run-on sentence. By dropping the article, the fragment is created, which causes the proper syntactical break.

Sometimes it is the reader who is allowed to designate which is the phrase and which is the fragment, as in this example:

gardenias
no matter where they are
dancing jazz music

One can feel the connectedness of "gardenias no matter where they are" as a phrase, or one can combine the last two lines to have: "no matter where they are dancing jazz music." Yet the sensitive ear will hear the tiniest comma after "gardenias," thus making this the fragment.

This brings us around to the articles, and you may have already guessed the guideline for using them. In the fragment you can often dispense with the use of an article, leaving the noun to stand alone.

Sometimes you can even erase the preposition from the fragment, especially if you are feeling that you are tired of reading haiku which begin with "in the garden." This guideline asks for sensitivity. It is not a hard and fast rule. But during the revising stage of writing your haiku, it is something to try. Cover up, and consider deleting, the preposition and article in the fragment and see if the haiku holds together. Perhaps it will even be stronger! If you feel the article and preposition are needed, then by all means use them. Do whatever works for your voice.

But if you are seeking to shorten the poem, look first to the fragment as you begin to cross out unneeded words.

However, one cannot follow the same rule in writing the phrase portion of the haiku. Sometimes critics make the comment in a workshop that a haiku is *choppy*.

> also green
> the spring-flooded meadow
> a snowy egret

What they are referring to is the feeling that at the end of each line the break in syntax is final. The two lines of the phrase are not hooked together in a flow of grammar and meaning. Reread the above haiku while adding "in" to the second line. Can you feel how the words smooth out the trip of the tongue?

> low winter sun
> raspberry leaves
> red and green

If to this "grocery-list haiku" we add a preposition and an article, we get:

> low winter sun
> in the raspberry leaves
> red and green

It pays to be aware of which two lines you wish to make into the phrase. It helps to read the two lines of a haiku that are to become your phrase aloud to see how they sound in your mouth and ears. If there is a too-clear break between the lines, ask yourself if you need to insert an article or an article plus a preposition. If you do, forget brevity and allow yourself the lyric pleasure of a smooth shift between these two lines. If I had chosen to make the first line the fragment, I would write the haiku as:

> low winter sun
> raspberry leaves glow
> red and green

Here, adding a verb gives the proper grammatical flow between lines two and three. If one added "in the" to the first line, the poem would read as "in the low winter sun raspberry leaves glow red and green," which to my ears would negate the fragment-phrase concept.

One other variation on this subject is the haiku in which the break occurs in the middle of the second line. Often one finds this in translations of Bashō's *haikai* (HI-KI, links taken out of a renga), which are two-liners set into three lines. Occasionally one will find an English haiku written in this manner. Again, it is often the result of a link being pulled out of a renga or a haiku written by a person using a 5-7-5 syllable count who ends up with too many images.

How Time Works in Haiku

Another universally agreed upon aspect of the haiku is that it is written in the present tense, so the reader has the feeling that the observed event is happening right now. In truth, one cannot write about the present, since one is always the observer setting down something that occurred in the past, even if it was only a few seconds ago. The feeling is so strong that all we truly have is the present, this very moment, that when we begin to think about the past, the present, and the future, we either come to the conclusion that "now" does not exist (because it has already become the past) or that there is no past nor future but only a continuous "now." Still, our language offers us several possibilities of time placement for what we write.

When most of our poetry was involved with the re-telling of past events or even legends and stories, it was accepted that one spoke of them as having happened in the past. Yet, at some point, it was discovered that a tale was more gripping if the storyteller made the audience feel that the events were unfolding in that very moment.

And since haiku is an interactive collaboration—the writer is attempting to lead the reader to experience a past event in this moment—it makes perfect sense that the poem places the action in the present tense.

In addition to the option of using the present tense of verbs, English also has a continuing present form, which is called a gerund and is formed by adding "ing" to a verb. A strange little prejudice has built up against the use of this verb form. Because the Japanese language does not have a similar verb form, early Japanese haiku authorities spoke out against the use of the gerund in English. Thus, one of the early laws of haiku was that we should restrict our use of it.

The only real problem that the gerund causes in English haiku is when more than one is used. The "ing" sound is so strong that when two or more verbs have it (raining, shining), along with perhaps an adjective (dazzling, amazing), in addition to a noun that accidentally ends in "ing" (morning, evening), the haiku can seem overburdened with the strong, repeated sound.

Some people have a natural tendency to use gerunds more than others. For them, one of the rewriting chores is to count the occurrences of "ing" in the verse. It has developed that some authors tend to use a gerund when the verb in the haiku refers to an action taken by a human—perhaps because in their vision of the incident they were doing and not just observing.

Many cultures have developed their languages without the form of "to be." Thus, they would not think of saying, "I am sad," but would reduce the importance of self while at the same time elevating the importance of the emotion with a more picturesque speech by saying, "Sadness comes to my doorstep." It is only with the increased emphasis on the individual in a society, and an increased self-awareness, that the verb form of "being" was formed. The advantage of the "be" form (I am, you are, we are, I have been, I will be) is that it allows a shortcut to an accurate accounting of a report of an individual. But in a poetry form like haiku, that minimalizes the importance of humanity, and emphasizes the outer world, dropping the egocentric mode of expression automatically places the poem closer to the realm of eternal nature.

The Place of Nature

In descriptions of what a haiku is, there is usually the mention that it is a poem about nature. This idea seems so innocent and easily understood that it is hard to comprehend the furious ink battles which have raged over this aspect of haiku. In trying to draw a clear line between humanity and nature, the authorities have discovered that there is none. It is fairly obvious that trees, clouds, and flowers are considered as nature and, thus, appropriate subjects for haiku.

For the Japanese, with their built-in humility and inborn self-effacement, it was easy and comfortable for them to place the emphasis of the poem outside of themselves in the glories of nature. We must all face the idea that we as persons will die, but nature, because it is able to renew itself, is everlasting. Therefore, to place the emphasis of one's poem within the larger picture of the ongoing world of nature is to assure that the subject matter of the poem lives and remains viable for the reader even in the future. Yet, over the years, more and more modern Japanese haiku contain human activities, and even feelings, opinions, and judgments of the author. For those writers without the classical sense of humility, it was hard to keep the happenings of humanity out of haiku. Today one can barely comprehend the furor that rose when Yamaguchi Seishi dared, in 1933, to write a haiku that contained such a modern and urban image as a locomotive, in spite of the sentiment in his haiku that praises nature.

Some English writers, though they have more easily accepted the products of humanity into their haiku, still have a hard time accepting a haiku that mentions humans. These people seem to want to draw a line between nature and humankind as if we were not a part of nature, but something outside of it or on the opposite side of it. So ingrained is the idea that a haiku is a poem about nature alone that some magazines automatically and autocratically separate the poems according to whether a reference to humanity appears in it or not.

The reason for doing this is a mistaken belief that they are following a Japanese ideal. From somewhere they have learned about the Japanese genre called *senryū*—SEN-RE-YOU—and have the idea that senryū are satire about the foibles of human experience, which they are. What they forget is the fact that Japanese haiku also contain references to humanity in them. The thing they do not understand is that there is a difference in tone between senryū and haiku. Since judging something as abstract as "tone" can never be completely agreed upon, and since English haiku give no indication of being something else other than haiku except by their form, some persons try to confuse the matter by clinging to a terminology that has no meaning for us.

These persons, who use the term senryū in conjunction with haiku, attempt to create a barrier between what they view as different kinds of haiku instead of accepting that a haiku can have as many variations in subject matter and atmosphere as there are writers. For a time, in English haiku history, it was thought that a senryū was a failed or inadequate haiku. Combined with this misconception was the practice by some persons of labeling other authors' work in a pejorative manner by calling it senryū simply because there was a human, or human action, in the haiku. For years, one magazine ritually segregated haiku with references to humanity in a separate section. Because other editors did not really know the reason for the difference between the two terms for English haiku, they published all their chosen haiku under both designations, just to be sure they had all bases covered.

In Japan, it is clear to anyone that a senryū is a haiku-like verse that lacks a *kigo* or season word. Because the senryū grew out of the practice of the *maekuzuke* (MY-COO-ZOO-KAY)—a game of poetry in which bar patrons attempted to write a response link to a poet's *hokku* based on vulgarity and saloon humor—the genre is yet today seen as being much less a high art than haiku. Haiku are signed with the author's name; senryū are not—for obvious reasons.

Because, when haiku was brought to English, we were not given the guideline that haiku had to always have a seasonal reference, we believed that whatever was written in three lines could be considered a haiku, whether it contained one of the regulation season words or phrases or not. And because of English's long literary history of poetry from and about humanity, it was very hard for us to write without a focus on persons, their activities, and the implements of their existence. Thus, from the beginning, many English haiku have focused on the actions of humans—sometimes to the exclusion of a mention of nature—and still, the proper name for the work is haiku.

The Art of Sensual Images

Your five or six senses are your basic tools for writing haiku. Haiku should come from what you have experienced and not what you think. Haiku depend on words that create the images the reader can see in his or her mind's eye. You might think that all words stand for something—and this is true—but many of our most-used words in poetry stand for ideas: wisdom, love, desire, fear, anger, longing, knowledge, beauty. These are also called abstractions because they are concepts—products of intelligence and not names of actual things one can verify with a sense.

Not only do haiku use mostly nouns to work with the names of things, they work best with what is lamely called the "thingness" of things. This is a real abstraction! But what it means is: instead of presenting the idea of a thing, or using the concepts of what something means to us, the author simply presents the thing as it is. Seeing the world in a grain of sand is not in haiku territory. Seeing sand as sand is. Instead of using things to talk about ideas or fantasy or imagination, the writer just writes about the thing as it is.

An easy way to get to this point is to avoid using adjectives and adverbs. There is a proverb: "calling a spade a spade." This works for haiku, also. Haiku do not tell the reader what to think, but show the things that will lead the reader along the path the author's mind has traveled.

This does not mean that there are no abstractions in haiku. They do use the abstract of time: morning or evening; the abstract of space: near or far; the abstract of size or measurement: large or small; and the abstract of memory or thinking. But any of these aspects should only constitute one-third—or one line—of the haiku. The other two-thirds of the haiku should be names or images of things the reader can see, hear, smell, taste, touch, or perceive.

The Importance of Simplicity

With this goal of directness in haiku is included the practice of saying things simply. At various times in our poetical history, it has been fashionable to find tropes or figures of speech to make poetry more lyrical. Instead of using the common noun as the name of a thing, the poet uses a new appellation, such as calling the ocean "mother of us all" or writing of the wind as the "messenger of the gods." As charming as this practice can be in small amounts, in large doses it can seem pompous and overblown. By speaking simply, the reader is allowed to form his or her own associations, memories, and ideas instead of being corralled into a narrow path someone else's wit has made.

Solving the Problem of Personalization

In this same vein, it is said that haiku also avoids the use of the Western poetical device of personalizing non-human things. To say a brook "smiles" would be seen as personifying a stream of water and therefore presenting the thing as more than what it is—just a stream of water.

This is a very tricky rule because we so easily accept that a brook runs, leaps, and even has a mouth! Our language has been personifying things for so long that it is practically impossible for us to rid ourselves of this concept. How easily we speak of the "leg of a chair" or the "head of the bed"—so nouns as well as verbs can personify objects. How does one decide when the author has committed the sin of personification? It depends on language customs and personal vision. If the verbs are customarily shared by humanity and a thing, you as author cannot be accused of personification.

If, however, you make up a new way of speaking of a thing—"the sun eyes the earth"—the jolt of this creativity will interrupt the normal low-key delivery of haiku. You are no longer speaking of the thing as it is but of how it is perceived by your intelligence.

For the lyrical poet, trained and charmed by the creation of figures of speech, haiku can either seem plain and painfully bare or delightfully simple and refreshing.

Finding a Common Language

Another aspect of keeping the language of a haiku simple and direct is the practice, in Japanese, of not using foreign words. It would seem that for English writers this would be fairly easy since we are so often accused of never having to learn a second language. But especially in haiku, when referring to things Japanese, how easily do words like *satori, zazen, tofu*, slip into our haiku? When this happens, a group of readers not acquainted with these terms is excluded from sharing the full sense of the poem. This is not a good thing. Then the poem is exclusive instead of inclusive. We do have English words for each foreign concept, so be writer enough to find the proper term. Haiku should be accessible, open to being understood by anyone, so that they form a common bond between us all—adult or child.

The Power of Positive Attitudes

Though not every haiku writer follows the ideal, there once was the idea that haiku should accentuate the positive instead of the negative. Using the word "not" in a haiku was seen as an error in keeping to the sunny side of the street—where haiku is supposed to be. As haiku writers have dipped into current events as inspiration for their work, this ideal has slowly slipped away. Still, if you are choosing entries for a contest from your haiku, it would be wise to leave aside those with dark or depressing images or ones stated in a negative manner. If one follows the haiku attitude of being nonjudgmental, this is less apt to appear in one's poems.

Ridding Yourself of Rhyme

Early translators of haiku, recognizing that this foreign form was poetry and wishing to make Japanese poetry seem more like English poetry, tried to form the English translation into rhymed lines. The most celebrated proponent of this style was Harold Stewart in his books: *A Net of Fireflies* and *A Chime of Windbells* (1960). The popularity of his attempt remains in the fact that, in 1986, *A*

Net of Fireflies was in its twenty-fifth printing. He set his versions, under a title, in a couplet with the two lines ending in a rhyme.

THE END OF AUTUMN

Autumn evening: on a withered bough,
A solitary crow is sitting now.*

Many people who know much about haiku react in exaggerated horror at this work, because in order to accomplish this radical change the translator has to add extraneous information or make changes in the original line order that can destroy the understanding of the technique the author was using.

The use of rhyme in haiku is not that far wrong when one understands that in Japanese, due to the constructive use of the vowels in the language, one has a one-in-six chance that any two lines will rhyme. Thus, the Japanese haiku often have not only a line-end rhyme but often one or more internal rhymes. The writers used this ability to strengthen their poems. Since rhyme occurs so easily it is easier to ignore, because the syntax is not shaped to cause the rhyme as must be done in English. As in the example above, one can feel and see where the translator made a change to get the rhyme.

It can happen that a person's first version of a haiku will naturally contain a rhyme. At this point the author can decide whether to keep it or to find synonyms to avoid the rhyme.

---

* Harold Stewart. *A Net of Fireflies*. Boston and Tokyo: Charles E. Tuttle Co., Inc., 1960, p. 88.

One thing to think about in making this decision is the feeling that when lines end with a matching rhyme, there is a feeling of the poem "closing down" or seeming to be finished. We are so used to having rhymes occur at the end of a line that when the ear hears the rhyme, the mind automatically signals that the poem is ended. In haiku, we want exactly the opposite effect—the poem should open out, leaving something else to be thought. The reader should carry the words farther—to continue to think about them, to ponder what has been said in order to arrive at a personal understanding of the poem.

Also, when a series of haiku are rhymed, their very shortness will lead to a singsong feeling of repetition that quickly becomes monotonous. Because English is a rhyme-poor language, our options for rhyme are greatly curtailed, leaving us with fewer choices than other languages.

For these reasons, and to separate haiku from the styles of Western poetry, it has always been a basic rule that haiku are not rhymed.

Managing Punctuation

Part of the drive toward brevity and simplicity in haiku has been the practice of reducing the use of punctuation. Because haiku are not sentences, many people maintain that they do not need to try to look like something they are not. There seems to be, at the moment, a continuum of those who use all the punctuation they can, often beginners, and those who use absolutely none. Those persons using some punctuation in their haiku will often find themselves making a dash after the fragment and hopefully nothing else, not even a comma in the middle of the phrase, even if there is a breath of the possibility of one. Sometimes the haiku will sound like a run-on sentence because the author is too lazy to rewrite the fragment clearly and thus *has* to add a dash, forcing the reader into the obligatory break.

For me, this is a red flag that the writer didn't stay with the rewrite long enough to solve the problem properly. Frankly, I see most punctuation as a cop-out. Almost any haiku written as a run-on sentence, with or without its dash, can be rewritten so that the syntax forms the one necessary break. Or the author can form places where the reader can decide where to make the break and thus give the haiku additional meaning. From this philosophy, I view haiku with punctuation as haiku which fail to fit this basic form.

You may find a haiku written in one line instead of three lines. A few authors defend their method as being an imitation of the Japanese method. The problem for beginners who follow this practice appears with the next haiku rule. If the author has a well-developed feeling for fragment and phrase, the grammar will show it. In these cases, my feeling is—why not write the haiku in the three lines so it shows the way it sounds.

Occasionally a haiku is so full of possible divisions into what is the fragment or the phrase that writing it in one line is the only way that offers the reader the complete freedom to find the breaks. And with each new arrangement the meaning of the poem varies. An example would be:

mountain heart in the stone tunnel light

Over the years I gradually gave up, and easily abandoned, the dashes, semicolons, commas and periods in order to incorporate ambiguity in the haiku, but it has been hard for me to let go of the question mark—which is rather silly, as it is so clear from the grammar that a question is being asked. Still, and yet . . . I mention this, so newcomers to haiku understand that rules are not written in stone, but something each of us has to work out for ourselves. It is an ongoing job, and one that, I hope, will never end.

The Use of Capital Letters

As writers have become more comfortable and knowledgeable about composing haiku, they have seen that a haiku is not a sentence and have slowly come to the realization that it perhaps should not be treated like one. In an effort to simplify the written poem, many writers have abandoned the initial capital letter that usually begins a sentence. Thus, at this time, the continued use of caps has become an indication of either a haiku beginner who carries on the practice from previous poetry writing or someone who refuses to rethink the changes the form has made.

Most people have been able to give up the period at the end of the poem rather easily because they see so clearly that the haiku is not a sentence and should not close down. Still, there are persons who are unable to stop using the initial capital letter. It seems more a reflex out of habit than a carefully thought-through technique.

Some persons, believing that the use of "i" for the personal pronoun "I" represents the proper haiku humility, have adopted this practice. It may work for them, but for others the jerk and jolt feeling that occurs when seeing the wrong use of "I" seems to add importance to the human element by deliberately calling attention to it. Others have taken the need for commonness to the point that all words within the haiku are written without caps, including days and months and proper names and places.

Writers who do retain the caps of proper names are often confused about whether to capitalize the names of the season (usually they are not) and of species of animals and flowers (again, usually not).

Six Basic Haiku Rules

Because haiku is a form genre—a kind of poetry that is built on certain rules—one must adopt some rules in order to write it. There are several ways of deciding which rules to use in writing haiku.

One can join a group whose leader proposes a set of rules that is agreeable to you. If you follow this person, you will have a ready-built audience who agrees with you completely about what a haiku is. It can be very comforting to share agreement with a group that is united under one goal with a loyal attachment to a leader. Often these masters are rather autocratic, but for some persons this kind of leadership lends credence to their goals. Commonly the leader of these groups also publishes a magazine so that the members of the group could be assured of fairly easy publication, which is sometimes not the case with haiku in poetry magazines. In this way, the student is competently led along a certain path, and the leader could take some pride in having a certain number of writers who not only agree with his or her rules but also extend haiku literature in this chosen style—which is very ego-gratifying. In these days of the Internet, it is possible to find Web sites led by persons who expend a great deal of energy and time on promoting their idea of what a haiku is. They are willing to teach beginners their methods, defend them against all other theories, and offer a system of sharing the poems among the like-minded.

Because, at some level, haiku is related to a spiritual practice, some of these masters espouse their theories with a religious fervor, and the groups take on many of the aspects of a church. In the same way that some persons are most comfortable within an organized religion, the same is true for haiku writers.

Another way to find out the rules one wants to follow is by reading the work of others and deciding which poems one admires the most. Then, consciously or unconsciously, the new writer begins to imitate that style which was created by a certain set of rules.

Very often persons feel that if they are going to learn a new genre, such as haiku, they will first study the old Japanese masters and follow their example. In many aspects this is a wise decision except for the reality that most translations are transliterations—not the words of the original.

This results in a stilted style similar to that of persons who write poetry based on inspiration of the Bible so that those poems result in using King James grammar such as "thou" and "hath." Yet today many translations follow the archaic rules of poetry, which the translator learned in grade school, instead of offering the haiku as they truly are, in word-for-word cases or in the context of modern poetry.

For those of you just beginning to learn haiku in today's world, doesn't it seem advantageous to follow the form as defined by today's usage and in your own language? To do this you need to read what other poets are doing with the form by purchasing an anthology to study and serve as inspiration. Out of this, your own set of rules will evolve. That does not mean this is the only way to write a haiku, but it should be seen as a starting place for your own thinking and exploration.

There is, thank goodness, no one way to write a haiku. Though the literature contains haiku that we admire and even model our own works on, there is no single style or technique which is absolutely the best. Haiku is too large for that. Haiku has, in its short history, been explored and expanded by writers so that we now have a fairly wide range of styles, techniques, and methods to investigate.

Usually writers stay with a rule until a new one is found to replace it. Because there are so many rules, we all have a different set with which we are working. You need to make the decision: are those rules, goals, or guidelines some I want for myself? This thought is much more gentle to the Universe than saying some haiku are good and others are bad.

You may have heard Robert Frost's saying that "poetry without rules is like a tennis match without a net." This is true also for haiku. If you are at that stage, a starting set of rules could be:

1. Write in three lines that are short, long, short without counting syllables.
2. Make sure the haiku has a fragment and a phrase.
3. Have some element of nature.
4. Use verbs in the present tense.
5. Avoid capital letters or punctuation.
6. Avoid rhymes.

As soon as you get proficient with these, you may feel your haiku all sound and look alike. Then it's time to raise the tennis net by picking a new rule or so, either from this list, or the much longer one at the end of this chapter. You can even make up your own rules decided upon from reading and admiring other haiku, or, and this is possible and not treason, from other poetry genres.

Twenty-Four Valuable Techniques

In the early years of English haiku writing, the prevalent credo how to write haiku was, sometimes implied and occasionally expressed, as being: if the author's mind/heart was correctly aligned in the "proper" attitude, while experiencing a so-called "haiku moment," one merely had to report on the experience to have a worthy haiku.

One reason for rejoicing in the acceptance of this view was that it bypassed the old 5-7-5 barrier crisis. Another advantage of this system of defining a haiku was that it bestowed near-religious honor on the author of an acceptable haiku. No one knew exactly why a particular haiku was *good*, but it was clear from the haiku that the author had experienced a moment of enlightenment (or *satori* for the Zen-inspired). If the moment was holy and the form fit the "philosophy" of the group publishing the verse, the haiku was said to be an excellent one.

Another plus for this viewpoint was that it allowed endless articles to be written for magazines on the Zen aspects of haiku writing, and even fuzzier articles on how to prepare for, find, recognize, and advertise one's haiku moments. Books were even compiled around this semi-religious idea.

However, many persons recognized that haiku moments were very much like other flashes of inspiration which, when transported into other media, became paintings, stories, dreams, or even new color schemes or recipes.

And many others shared the frustration of having a truly life-altering moment of insight and then never being able to write a decent haiku that expressed the wonder and majesty of that moment. They would ask, what was wrong with me? Was I not spiritually prepared enough? Was I too common? Too inattentive? Too word-numb? Maybe too many of my own religious beliefs kept me from the Zen nirvana of haiku?

The truth is: probably all of the above can change one's ability to write good haiku. Ouch, that hurts. However, I felt a sense of rescue when I came across the little booklet *Aware: A Haiku Primer,* written by hand and illustrated by Betty Drevniok, who was at the time she wrote the book (in the early 80s I am guessing as it has no date) president of the Haiku Society of Canada. Among the many great tips for writing haiku, and obtaining the questionable Zenniness of Zen, was her precept: "Write [haiku] in three short lines using the principle of comparison, contrast, or association." On page 39 she used an expression that had not appeared in all the other discussions of haiku: "This technique provides the pivot on which the reader's thought turns and expands." Technique! So there are tools one can use, I thought joyfully.

And I practiced her methods with glee and relative (to me) success and increased enjoyment. Suddenly I could figure out by myself what was wrong with a haiku that failed to jell as I thought it should. I could ask myself if there was a *comparison,* a *contrast* or an *association* between the images and if this relationship was clear and understandable to the reader.

Slowly, over the years, I found by doing my own translations of the old Japanese masters, and from the haiku of my contemporaries, that there were more factors than just these three on which one could build a haiku. However, there seemed a disinterest among other persons wanting to study these aspects, which I call techniques. Perhaps this is because in the haiku scene there continues to be such a reverence for the haiku moment and such a dislike for what are called desk haiku.

The definition of a desk haiku is a verse written from an idea or from simply playing around with words instead of the direct result of an experience. The idea was that if you don't experience an event with all your senses, it is not valid haiku material. A haiku from your mind was intellectual, and very likely to be half dead and unrealistic. An experienced writer could only smile at such naiveté, but the label of desk haiku was the death knell for any haiku declared as such. This fear made people new to the scene afraid to work with techniques or even the idea that techniques were needed in writing down the elusive haiku moment.

At the risk of leading you into the quasi-sin of writing dreaded desk haiku, I would like to discuss and illustrate some of the haiku writing techniques which I have recognized and used.

1. The Technique of Comparison—In the words of Betty Drevniok: "In haiku the SOMETHING and the SOMETHING ELSE are set down together in clearly stated images. Together they complete and fulfill each other as ONE PARTICULAR EVENT." She leaves it to the reader to understand that the idea of comparison is showing how two different things are similar or share similar aspects.

> a spring nap
> downstream cherry trees
> in bud

What is expressed, but not said, is the thought that buds on a tree can be compared to flowers taking a nap. One could also ask to what other images could cherry buds be compared? A long list of items can form in one's mind and be substituted for the first line. Or one can turn the idea around and ask what in the spring landscape can be compared to a nap without naming things that close their eyes to sleep. By changing either of these images one can come up with one's own haiku while getting a new appreciation and awareness of the function of comparison.

2. The Technique of Contrast—Now the job feels easier. All one has to do is to contrast images.

> long hard rain
> hanging in the willows
> tender new leaves

The delight from this technique is the excitement that opposites create. You have instant built-in interest in the most common haiku moment. And yet most of the surprises of life are the contrasts, and therefore this technique is a major one for haiku.

3. The Technique of Association—This can be thought of as "how different things relate or come together." The Zen of this technique is called "oneness," or showing how everything is part of everything else. You do not have to be a Buddhist to see this; simply being aware of what *is*, is illumination enough.

> moving
> a handful of moonlight
> the owl's wing

The main association is between "hand" and "wing," with a minor one between "owl" and "moonlight." The several "o" sounds also add to the continuation of associations.

4. The Technique of the Riddle—This is probably one of the very oldest poetical techniques. It has been guessed that early spiritual knowledge was secretly preserved and passed along through riddles. Because poetry, as it is today, is basically the commercialization of religious prayers, incantations, and knowledge, it is no surprise that riddles still form a serious part of poetry's transmission of ideas.

> where do they go?
> these flowers on a path
> by summer's passing

The trick is to state the riddle in as puzzling terms as possible. What can one say that the reader cannot figure out the answer? The more intriguing the setup and the better the correlation between the images, the better the haiku seems to work. Here, as in anything, you can overextend the joke and lose the reader completely.

Oh, the old masters' favorite tricks with riddles were "is that a flower falling or is it a butterfly?" or "is that snow on the plum branch or blossoms?" and the all-time favorite—"am I a butterfly dreaming I am a man or a man dreaming I am a butterfly?" Again, if you wish to experiment, you can ask yourself the question: if I saw snow on a branch, what else could it be besides blossoms? Or seeing a butterfly going by, you ask yourself what else besides a butterfly could you have caught in the corner of your eye?

5. The Technique of Sense-switching—This is another old-time favorite of the Japanese haiku masters, but one they have used very little and with a great deal of discretion. It is simply to speak of the sensory aspect of a thing and then change to another sensory organ. Usually it involves hearing something one sees or vice versa or to switch between seeing and tasting. Some persons have this ability naturally—it is called synesthesia. The most famous example of this is Bashō's "old pond" haiku:

old pond
a frog jumps into
the sound of water

Here, the frog does not jump into the water but into the sound of water. The mind puzzle this haiku creates is how to separate the frog from the water, the sound of water from the water, the frog from the sound it will make entering the water, and the sound from the old pond. It cannot be done because all these factors are one, but the reader arrives at this truth through the jolt of having the senses scrambled.

6. The Technique of Narrowing Focus—This is a device that was often used by the Japanese master Buson because he, being an artist, was a very visual person. Basically what you do is to start with a wide-angle lens on the world in the first line, switch to a normal lens for the second line, and zoom in for a close-up in the end. It sounds simple, but when done well it is very effective in bringing the reader's attention down to one basic element or fact of the haiku.

the whole sky
in a wide field of flowers
one tulip

7. The Technique of Using a Metaphor—I can just hear those of you who have had some training in haiku, sucking in your breath in horror. There *is* that ironclad rule that one does not use metaphor in haiku. Posh. As you can see, Bashō used it, and used it perfectly, in his most famous "crow haiku."

> on a bare branch
> a crow lands
> autumn dusk

What he was saying, in other words, was that the way darkness comes down on an early autumn evening is the way it feels when a crow lands on a bare branch. I never truly understood this hokku until late one day, when I was leaning against the open door of my tiny writing hut. Lost in thought, I was so still that I excited my resident crow's curiosity, causing him to fly down suddenly to land about two feet from my cheek on a thin, nearly bare, pine branch. I felt the rush of darkness coming close, as close as an autumn evening and as close as a big black crow. The thud of his big feet hitting the bare branch caused the tiny ripple of anxiety one has when it gets dark so early in the autumn. In that moment I felt I knew what Bashō had experienced. It is extremely hard to find a haiku good enough to place up against Bashō's rightly famous one, so I'll pass on giving you an example of my haiku. But this is a valid technique and one that can bring you many lovely and interesting haiku. Haiku is poetry, and it does use another of poetry's oldest tools—the metaphor. Feel free to use metaphor in your haiku—just use it the way the Japanese have taught us to do.

8. The Technique of Using a Simile—Usually, in English, you know a simile is coming when you spot the words "as" and "like." Occasionally one will find in a haiku the use of a simile with these words still wrapped around it, but the Japanese have proved to us that this is totally unnecessary. From them we have learned that it is enough to put two images in juxtaposition (next to each other) to let the reader figure out the "as" and "like" for him/herself. Basically the unspoken rule is that you can use simile, which the rule-sayers also warned us against, if you are smart enough to simply drop the "as" and "like." Besides, by doing this you give readers some active part that makes them feel very smart when they discover the simile for themselves.

> strawberry
> another red tongue
> on mine

9. The Technique of the Sketch or Shiki's *Shasei*— Though this technique is often given Shiki's term *shasei* (sketch from life) or *shajitsu* (reality), it has been in use since the beginning of poetry in the Orient. The poetic principle is "to depict the thing just as it is." The reason Shiki took it up as a poetical cause, and thus made it famous, was his own rebellion against the many other techniques used in haiku. Shiki was, by nature it seemed, against whatever was the status quo—a true rebel. If older poets had overused any idea or method, it was his personal goal to point this out and suggest something else. This was followed until someone else got tired of it and suggested something new. This seems to be the way poetry styles go in and out of fashion.

Thus, Shiki hated associations, contrasts, comparisons, wordplays, puns, and riddles—all the things you are learning here! He favored the quiet simplicity of just stating what he saw without anything else happening in the haiku. He found the greatest beauty in the common sight, simply reported exactly as it was seen, and ninety-nine percent of his haiku were written in his style. Many people still feel he was right. There are some moments that are perhaps best said as simply as possible in his way. Yet, Shiki himself realized in 1893, after writing very many haiku in this style, that used too much, even his new idea could become lackluster. So the method is *an* answer, but never the complete answer of how to write a haiku.

> evening
> waves come into the cove
> one at a time

10. The Technique of Double Entendre (or Double Meanings)—Anyone who has read translations of Japanese poetry has seen how much poets delighted in saying one thing and meaning something else. Often only translators knew the secret language and got the jokes that may or may not be explained in footnotes. In some cases the pun was to cover up a sexual reference by speaking of something ordinary in such a way that its hidden meaning could be found by the initiated. There are whole lists of words with double meanings—spring rain = sexual emissions, and jade mountain = the Mound of Venus. But we have the same devices in English also, and haiku can use them in the very same way.

> hills
> touching each other
> at the river

Here the ambiguity of the haiku can be taken as the reality that "when hills touch it is at a river" or one can think "out in the hills at the river a couple are touching each other." Or "on the hills of their bodies, a couple are touching each other in the wettest places."

11. The Technique of Using Puns—Again we can only learn from the master punsters—the Japanese. We have the very same opportunities in English, but we haiku writers may not be as well-versed as the Japanese in using them because there have been periods of Western literary history when this overworked skill has been looked down upon. And even though the *hai* of haiku means "joke, or fun, or unusual," there are still writers whose faces freeze into a frown when encountering a pun in three lines.

> a sign
> at the fork in the road
> "fine dining"

12. The Technique of Wordplay—Again, we have to admit the Japanese do this best. Their work is made easier by the fact that many of their place names have double meanings and many of their words are homonyms—words that sound the same but have different meanings. Still, we also have many words with multiple meanings, and there is no reason we cannot learn to explore our own language. A good look at many of our cities' names could give new inspiration: Oak-land, Anchor Bay, Ox-ford, Cam-bridge. Especially the descriptive names of plants, animals, and things have opportunity for haiku in them.

> yellow sticks
> writing a desert poem
> pencil cholla

13. The Technique of Verb/Noun Exchange—This is a very gentle way of doing wordplay and getting double duty out of words. In English we have many words which function as both verbs and nouns. By constructing the poem carefully, one can utilize both aspects of such words as leaves/going away, spots/sees, flowers/blossoms, sprouts/pushes out, greens/leafy vegetables, fall/autumn, spring/coiled wire, and hundreds more. You can use this technique to say things that are not allowed in haiku. For instance, one would not be admired for saying that "the willow tree strings raindrops" because it makes a personification of a thing of nature, but one can get away with making it sound as if the strings of willow are really the spring rain manifested in raindrops. This is one of those cases where the reader has to decide which permissible stance the writer has taken.

spring rain
the willow strings
raindrops

14. The Technique of Close Linkage—Basically this could come as a subtopic to the techniques of association, but since it also works with contrast and comparison, I like to give it its own rubric. In making any connection between the two parts of a haiku, the leap can be a small one, and even a well-known one. Usually beginners are easily impressed with close linkage and experiment first with the most easily understood examples of this form. They understand it and feel comfortable using the technique.

winter cold
finding on a beach
an open knife

15. The Technique of Leap Linkage—Then as a writer's skills increase, and as he or she reads many haiku, either their own or others, such easy leaps quickly fade in excitement. Being human animals, we seem destined to seek the next level of difficulty and to find new thrills. So the writer begins to attempt leaps that a reader new to haiku may not follow and therefore judge to be nonsense. The nice thing about this aspect is that when one begins to read haiku by a certain author, one will find some of the haiku simply meaningless, but years later, with many haiku experiences, the reader will discover the truth or poetry or beauty in a haiku that seemed dead and closed earlier. I think the important point in creating with this technique is that the writer should always be totally aware of his or her truth. Poets of the surrealistic often make leaps which simply seem impossible to follow—an example would be the work of Paul Celan, where the reader simply has to go on faith that the author knew what he was writing about. This is rare in haiku. Usually, if you think about the words long enough and deeply enough, you can find the author's truth.

leaping
a fish opens a door
in the lake

16. The Technique of Mixing It Up—What I mean here is mixing up the action so the reader does not know if nature is doing the acting or if a human is doing it. As you know, haiku are praised for getting rid of authors, authors' opinions, and authors' actions. One way to sneak this in is to use the gerund (suffix "ing" added to a verb) combined with an action that seems sensible for both a human and for the things in nature to do. Very often, when I use a gerund in a haiku, I am using shorthand to refer to an action that I have taken. This device minimizes the impact of the author's person but allows an interaction between humanity and nature.

end of winter
covering the first row
of lettuce seeds

17. The Technique of *Sabi* (SAH-BEE)—I almost hesitate to bring up this idea as a technique because the word *sabi* has taken on so many meanings over the innumerable years it has been in Japan, and now that it comes to the English language it is undergoing even more mutations. As fascinated as Westerners have become with the word, the Japanese have maintained for centuries that no one can really, truly comprehend what sabi really is, and thus they change its definition according to their moods. Some call sabi—beauty with a sense of loneliness in time, akin to, but deeper than, nostalgia. D.T. Suzuki maintains that sabi is "loneliness" or "solitude," but that it can also be "miserable," "insignificant," "pitiable," "asymmetry," and "poverty." Donald Keene sees sabi as "an understatement hinting at great depths." So you see, we are rather on our own with this. A split-rail fence sagging with overgrown vines has sabi; a freshly painted picket fence does not. That is how I think of it. As a technique, one puts together images and verbs which create this desired atmosphere. Often in English this hallowed state is sought by using the word "old" and by writing of cemeteries and grandmas. These English tricks wear thin quickly.

> listening ears
> petals fall into
> the silence

18. The Technique of *Wabi* (WAH-BEE)—This is the twin brother of sabi, which has just as many personas, that can be defined as poverty or beauty judged to be the result of living simply. Frayed and faded Levis have the wabi that bleached designer jeans can never achieve. Thus one can argue that the above haiku samples are really more wabi than sabi—and suddenly one understands the big debate. However, I offer one more haiku that I think is more wabi than sabi because it offers a scene of austere beauty and poignancy.

> parting fog
> on wind barren meadows
> birth of a lamb

19. The Technique of _Yūgen_ (YOU-GHEN)—This is another of these Japanese states of poetry which is usually defined as "mystery" and "unknowable depth." Somehow _yūgen_ has avoided the controversy of the other two terms. But since deciding which haiku exemplifies this quality is a judgmental decision, there is rarely consent over which verse has it and which does not. One could say a woman's face half-hidden behind a fan has yūgen. The same face half-covered with pink goo while getting a facial, however, does not. But still, haiku writers do use the atmosphere as defined by yūgen to make their words be a good haiku by forcing their readers to think and to delve into the everyday sacredness of common things.

> a swinging gate
> on both sides flowers
> open—close

20. The Technique of the Paradox—One of the aims of haiku is to confuse the reader just enough to attract interest. Using a paradox will engage interest and give the reader something to ponder after the last word. Again, one cannot use nonsense but has to construct a true, connected-to-reality paradox. It is not easy to come up with new ones or good ones, but when it happens, one should not be afraid of using it in a haiku.

> waiting room
> a patch of sunlight
> wears out the chairs

21. The Technique of the Improbable World—This is very close to paradox but has a slight difference. Again, this is an old Japanese tool which is often used to make the poet sound simple and childlike. It demonstrates a distorted view of science—one we know is not true, but always has the possibility of being true—as in quantum physics.

> evening wind
> colors of the day
> blown away

22. The Technique of Using Humor—This is the dangerous stuff. Because one has no way of judging another person's tolerance for wisecracks, jokes, slurs, bathroom and bedroom terminology, one should enter the territory of humor as if it is strewn with landmines. And yet, if one is reading before a live audience, nothing draws in the admiration and applause like a few humorous haiku. Very often the gentle humor of a haiku comes from citing the honest reactions of humankind. But some people will feel you have left the sacred realm of haiku to enter the less exalted world of senryū if there is any hint of humanity combined with humor. So choose your terms carefully, add to your situation with appropriate leaps, and may the haiku gods smile on you.

> dried prune faces
> guests when they hear
> we have only a privy

23. The Technique of "As Is Above: Is Below"—Though it seems to be using a religious precept, this technique is only working to make the tiny haiku a well-rounded thought. Simply said: the first line and the third line exhibit a connectedness or a completeness. Some say one should be able to read the first line and the third line to find it makes a complete thought. Sometimes one does not know in which order to place the images in a haiku. When the images in the first and third lines have the strongest relationship, the haiku usually feels balanced. As an exercise, take any haiku and switch the lines around to see how this factor works. Try reading the following haiku without the second line. See how "straight down" applies both to the rain and the horse's head.

> rain
> the horse's head bowed
> straight down

24. The Technique of Finding the Divine in the Common—This is a technique that seems to happen mostly without conscious control. A writer will make a perfectly ordinary and accurate statement about common things, but due to the combination of images and ideas and what happens between them, a truth will be revealed about the Divine. Since we all have various ideas about what the Divine is, two readers of the same haiku may not find the same truth or revelation in it. Here, again, the reader becomes a writer to find a greater truth behind the words.

smoke
incense unrolls
itself

Actually Getting A Haiku Written

If you are feeling overwhelmed by this mass of guide-lines, rules, and theories of haiku, it is time to take a pen-cil in hand to start writing your own haiku. So you stare at the wall and the pristine paper and nothing comes to mind? Here is an easy method of attaching training wheels to your haiku mind.

You simply start with a haiku someone else has writ-ten. Find one you really like, one that speaks to you, one that has an aspect you admire. Even if you already have written some haiku of your own, but admire a technique someone else is using, you can learn that method by try-ing this process. Or you can pick a haiku you feel is not quite right and needs some correcting or editing. Every-one loves to revise someone else's work! Go for it.

Take a sheet of unlined paper and turn it sideways so

it is wider than it is tall. At the left edge, near the top corner, write in bold print the first line of the haiku with which you have picked to work. In the center of the left margin, write the second line. Near the bottom of the sheet, above the lower left-hand corner, write the third line.

Now working one line at a time, see how many ways you can rewrite the information it contains by substituting other verbs and nouns. Write down whatever comes to your mind without thinking of whether your idea is good or not, relevant or not, fitting or not. Just let your inner self play with the words. If nothing happens, that is okay.

Go to the next line of the original haiku. Have you ever seen or experienced something similar? Can you write about this in a better way? Here you give yourself the satisfaction of scratching the itch to change what others have written. Enjoy it! Indulge yourself.

Sometime before the page is filled with the shine of your pencil, take a look at the last line of the original haiku. Does it fit with anything you have written? Or have you already found a better third line than this for one of your best ideas? Do you think that changing the last line of the original haiku could make it better? If so, write down the possibilities.

Then on a clean sheet of paper write your own haiku formed out of the sets of three lines as you have discovered them by thinking up your variations to the original haiku. Be sure that out of this assortment of possibilities you have your own haiku hiding somewhere on the page. Try out all the combinations. Take one of your suggestions for a third line and place it in the beginning of your new haiku. Pick a second line, from your many attempts, or if the idea comes to you, make up a new one.

Listening to your inner self is the most vital thing you can do at this stage. The haiku is there, you have already written it. You simply have to listen to your own directions in order to put it together the way it was inside of you. Do take the time to write down all the possible combinations of lines—even if that loudmouthed inner critic tries to tell you not to. Because you are not yet done with this haiku.

Save these worksheets because days or months later, when you look at them again, I can almost guarantee that some idea, phrase, or image will be the starting point for another of your haiku. This exercise is too rich to waste.

In studying the existing works of Bashō, one can see that before he wrote his now-famous "old pond" poem, he had used that last line—"the sound of water"—in two other verses in the previous months. In both of these cases the phrase was used in its usual sense. But still, something in him must have told him that there was more to be found in the line. So do not give up.

And think of trying this exercise again with another haiku. Anytime you are feeling blocked or want to write a haiku but have no moment of inspiration or ideas, this exercise will get your juices flowing. Precisely because haiku written in this manner do not come with the marvelous charge of inspiration, it is easier to test them, change them, rub out and polish them anew.

The results of such an exercise are called desk haiku by some persons because they are not written in response to a moment of inspiration. But it may be that working in this method you have recalled a moment of your past which has formed the basis for your new haiku. Then, technically, your desk haiku no longer deserves that name because it is the result of a delayed moment of inspiration. Learn to split frog hairs. Defend yourself.

A Checklist For Revising Haiku

While learning to write haiku it can be helpful to have a list so you can quickly check the new work for common errors. Until you make up your own list, you might want to borrow this one; it is the one I use for my work. Along with the points are included ways of making corrections.

1. Can you clearly see or hear the two distinct parts? If not, check where to add a preposition and/or article.
2. Does the haiku read like a sentence? By changing either the order of the words or the verb structure you can usually solve this problem.
3. What is the shape of the haiku? If you are counting syllables, are you sure you have the right numbers in each of the lines?
4. If the first or last line is the longest, could it fit better in the middle so the haiku has the shape you wish for it to have?
5. Are there pronouns in it? Do you really need them or can they be written out?
6. Are all the verbs in the present tense?
7. How many gerunds, or words ending in "ing," have you used?
8. Are there adverbs in the haiku? Do you really, really

need them to convey the sense of the thought?

9. Is there any word that could be removed without losing the sense of the verse?

10. Is there any word that could have another word substituted for it? There are so many similar words that one must be certain to use the one and only one that makes the haiku. Wiggle every word.

11. Poetry comes from exactitude. This means that instead of writing "tree" the author tells whether the tree is an oak or a pine tree. Appreciate the additional information that comes from associations of certain names —for example, "oak" suggests strength and endurance, and "pine" can also mean "to yearn for or long for"— and use these opportunities to enrich the haiku.

12. Does the haiku work on more than one level? Is it at once describing a scene and also a state of mind or being or a philosophy?

13. Can others understand your poem? If you are not sure, this is the time to show your haiku to others to see if they can understand it.

14. Have you read this haiku somewhere else? Have you unconsciously taken someone else's haiku for your own?

15. Does the haiku sing to you? Do you love repeating it to yourself? Does it totally delight you?

16. If not, if something bothers you about it, go back to the moment of inspiration, when you were given the idea for the haiku. Look around the scene to see if you have missed any vital details that need to be in your poem. Does the reworked poem still express your original feeling or idea?

17. Should this idea be expressed in a haiku? Does it need

more than one haiku to say it all? Should there be a series of haiku on the subject?

18. Could the idea or inspiration be better expressed in a tanka or another from of poetry?
19. Can it be stated in other ways? Take the time to write up all the variations that you think of. Save and honor them all.

Believe It or Not—More Rules

If you are still looking for more haiku rules to follow, here is a list of many that have come and gone over the years as well as the ones already discussed above. As you read them over, you will see how much you have already learned.

1. Write 5-7-5 syllables in the three lines.
2. Write lines of any length but have only seventeen syllables in the whole haiku.
3. Write seventeen syllables in one line.
4. Write seventeen syllables in a vertical (flush left or centered) configuration with one word on each line. This method makes one read the work more slowly because the eyes must travel back and forth so often.
5. Use less than seventeen syllables written in three horizontal lines as short, long, short.
6. Use less than seventeen syllables written in three vertical lines as short, long, short.
7. Write what can be said in one breath.
8. Use a season word (*kigo*) or seasonal reference.
9. Use a caesura at the end of either the first or second line, but not at both line ends.

10. Never have all three lines make a complete or run-on sentence.

11. Have two images that are only comparative when illuminated by the third image. Example: spirit retreat / cleaning first the black stove / and washing my hands

12. Have two images that are only associative when illuminated by the third image. Example: fire-white halo / at the moment of eclipse / your face

13. Have two images that are only in contrast when illuminated by the third image. Example: two things ready / but not touching the space between / fire

14. Always write in the present tense of here and now.

15. Make limited use, or non-use, of personal pronouns.

16. Use personal pronouns written in the lower case. Example: i am a . . .

17. Eliminate all the possible uses of gerunds ("ing" endings on verbs).

18. Study and check the articles. Do you use too many of the words "the" or "a," or too few? Are they all the same in one poem or are they varied?

19. Use common sentence syntax in both the phrase and the fragment.

20. Use three sentence fragments.

21. Study the order in which the images are presented (e.g., first the wide-angle view, then the medium range, and lastly the zoomed-in close-up).

22. Save the "punch line" for the end line.

23. Work to find the most fascinating and eye-catching first lines.

24. Write about ordinary things in an ordinary way using ordinary language.

25. Study Zen and let your haiku express the wordless way of making images.
26. Study any religion or philosophy and let this echo in the background of your haiku.
27. Use only concrete images.
28. Invent lyrical expressions for the image.
29. Attempt to have levels of meaning in the haiku. On the surface it is a set of simple images; underneath, a philosophy or lesson of life.
30. Use images that evoke simple rustic seclusion or accepted poverty. (*sabi*)
31. Use images that evoke classical, elegant separateness. (*shibumi*)
32. Use images that evoke nostalgic, romantic images of austere beauty. (*wabi*)
33. Use images that evoke a mysterious aloneness. (*yūgen*)
34. Use a paradox.
35. Use puns and wordplays.
36. Write of the impossible in an ordinary way.
37. Use only lofty or uplifting images—no war, blatant sex, crime, or local news.
38. Tell it as it is in the real world around us.
39. Use only images from nature with no mention of humanity.
40. Mix subjects of humans and nature.
41. Designate humans as non-nature and give all these non-nature haiku another name, such as senryū.
42. Avoid all reference to yourself.
43. Refer to yourself obliquely as the poet, this old man, or with a personal pronoun.
44. Use no punctuation for ambiguity.

45. Use all normal sentence punctuation.

    : = a full pause

    ; = a half stop or pause

    . . . = something left unsaid

    , = a slight pause

    – = saying the same thing in other words

    . = full stop

46. Capitalize the first word of every line.
47. Capitalize the first word only.
48. Capitalize proper names according to English rules.
49. All words in lower case.
50. All words in upper case.
51. Rewrite any rhymes.
52. Rhyme last words in the first and third lines.
53. Use rhymes in other places within the haiku.
54. Use alliteration—repetition of sounds—that relates to the subject matter in order to increase a certain feeling.
55. Use the words that you hear in your head only.
56. Always end the haiku with a noun.
57. Write haiku only from an "aha" moment.
58. Use any inspiration as a starting point to develop and write haiku.
59. Avoid too many, or nearly all, verbs.
60. Cut out prepositions (in, on, at, among, between) whenever possible, especially in the fragment.
61. Eliminate adverbs.
62. Don't use more than one modifier per noun. Their use should be limited to the absolute sense of the haiku.
63. Share your haiku by adding one at the close of your letters.

64. Treat your haiku like poetry; it's not a greeting card verse.
65. Write down every haiku that comes to you. Even the so-called bad ones. It may inspire the next one, which will surely be better.

Bashō had a motto: "Learn the rules; and then forget them." But first he said, "Learn the rules."

Preserving Your Haiku

Every writer needs a system of organizing their poems and stories. The smallness of haiku makes a workable arrangement even more imperative. Nothing is more frustrating than to know you wrote a certain haiku about a specific event and now be unable to recall the verse exactly or even find where it was written down. It is even more frustrating to work on a haiku in your head, get it perfectly right and then, by neglecting to write it down, have it lost forever. Like dreams, haiku have a way of vanishing; especially those thought of in the dark of night.

So the first rule of haiku is to always have paper and pencil close at hand. For some of us this means a pouch hangs from the mattress with pen, flashlight, and assorted papers. Clothes with pockets should be equipped with at least a folded sheet of paper and the stub of a pencil. Many persons devise tiny notebooks—stapled sheets of leftover paper into a covered booklet that best fits your pocket. Or you can make a science of finding the perfect companion for your haiku.

When out on walks, consider whether to take a pencil (the lead can break in your pocket) or a pen (which can suddenly go dry or leak into a stain). I have had all possibilities happen. Once I ended up writing down a haiku with a bit of charcoal from a beach fire on a piece of driftwood. Another time I was reduced to writing the haiku on smooth rocks, and photographing them (because the camera was working and the pen was not). I have also sharpened broken pencils on a rough rock, and have written haiku on my arm in ink when there was no paper.

The process of rewriting and the completely realistic danger of the little pocket notebook going through the laundry usually forces writers to also keep a more permanent record of their haiku.

Some people use index cards with one haiku per card. In this way all the versions of one haiku can be saved on a card or they can be separated onto individual cards. These cards need a system of numbering and of organization by subject or time so you can find the one haiku you are looking for later.

You can organize your poems by the five seasons. Each season is then divided into the categories of the season or its attributes: celestial—all the haiku about skies, weather, stars, planets; terrestrial—references to parts of the landscape; livelihood—human activities common to a certain season, including holiday activities; animals—ones associated with a certain season; and plants—ones that reflect the season. Within these seven categories one can arrange the subjects alphabetically.

Some persons copy their haiku into books in chronological order as they are written, giving each one a number and the date. Thus, if you remember writing that great haiku last August at the beach, you only need to flip back to August's cache of haiku. Some persons use ready-made journals to make a small book of their haiku written on a trip or around a special event.

The use of computers is an excellent way of organizing haiku. It is possible to create a database so you can search for the haiku by subject, first word, or date. Lacking those skills, one can always type up the haiku in series, title them, and save them under various descriptive headings. Typing up a haiku on a computer while using the copy and paste features makes it easy to revise while keeping the original version and still experimenting with new words from the thesaurus. Just don't get carried away by big words.

For those who are into journaling, nothing adds spice to the recounting of the day's activities like a haiku adding insight in the middle of the page. This is an excellent method of detailing in prose the background to the haiku material. You never know when you will begin to write *haibun* and need all of this information that you might have otherwise forgotten.

This talk about organizing your haiku cannot be complete without mentioning the ultimate way of organizing haiku—making your own book of haiku.

Chapter
Three

ENJOYING HAIKU
WITH OTHERS

Appearing at Poetry Readings

One of the most delightful ways of sharing haiku is to
have a friend who also enjoys reading and writing haiku.
If you can decipher the tone of your friend's voice, or the
poignant silence at the other end of the line, here is in-
stant help to know whether the verse works or not, and if
not, where the problem lies.

Another way of sharing haiku verbally is if two or
more persons go on what the Japanese call a *ginkō* (GING-
KOH). This is a walk that is usually planned in a special
place—a garden or area of scenic beauty—for the pur-
pose of being inspired with haiku. As the group strolls
along, people recite the haiku that come to mind. For
many Westerners, particularly the shy, it is easier to write
down the haiku and then when the group settles down
for a rest or cup of tea afterwards, to read the fresh new
haiku to them. How often, as the group shares what they
have written, has there been the thought, "Now I saw
that same phenomenon and never realized the possible
haiku in it."

Reading one's haiku to a small group of fellow haiku

writers is an excellent practice. Here, everyone has already honed their ability to hear and understand a haiku, so even the biggest leaps can be quickly and accurately understood and appreciated.

The ultimate experience of sharing your haiku verbally is to take part in a poetry reading. This is very different from sharing your haiku with a group of like-minded aficionados who understand how haiku work.

When it comes to planning for the big night of the local poetry reading, you could perhaps use some professional advice. Here are some suggestions given by Professor Jerome J. Cushman, a theatre director, actor, dancer, and recently retired professor from the Institute for the Deaf at the Rochester Institute of Technology, as put forth in his paper "Presenting Haiku: Considerations for the Oral Interpretation of Haiku." Because he is so helpful, the following is amply lifted from his kindly lent article.

"If time allows, fully memorize the haiku but having a script in view can help build confidence. Using large print with notations in different colors makes for easy reference if a word or idea slips the mind. Remember, whether presenting one haiku or several haiku as part of a longer lecture, these techniques can still be utilized."

His advice on vocal techniques is absolutely critical and deserves the time and patience of practice.

"Clear and appropriate pronunciation, articulation, phonation and resonation are important. Know the meanings of all the words in the poem and how to say them correctly. Say each part of every word clearly. Allow each sound to fully develop in the chest, head and mouth. A general rule is to clip the consonants and prolong the vowel sounds. This experience is not like 'one on one' conversation, so think of projecting the voice out to the audience.

"The meaning and emotion of the haiku comes from the appropriate variety of the pitch, pace, power and pause. The variation of pitch is the intonation and inflection in the voice. It is the song or highness and lowness of the tone. Monotone is boring. A sing song pattern is also boring. Variation of pitch is important for the audience's interest, understanding and emotional involvement.

"The pace is the speed at which the words are spoken and joined together into images. The presenter already has the ideas clearly in his or her mind. The audience needs the time to go through four steps for the effective communication of the poem. Each member of the audience needs to be able to 1) hear, 2) think, 3) react or feel, and 4) understand. If a presenter keeps this four-step process in mind then the audience will have time to appreciate the poem. Again, variety of the tempo is interesting."

Another method is to repeat each haiku in the beginning of the reading, and even later if a haiku is more difficult to understand. As the audience warms to the process, you can skip this on the easily understood or comprehended verses, especially those in a sequence where the sense of one verse easily leads to the next one.

"Vary the intensity and volume. These also help put the emphasis on the important words and the subordination of the less important words. Allowing proper pauses creates the phrasing and timing. Because haiku are short, take time to orally present each image appropriately."

It is possible to change the inflection and emphasis

within a haiku as you reread it so that an alternative meaning can be made clear. This always impresses audiences who think haiku are simple.

"As the interpretation is developed mark a script by underlining the words to be strongly emphasized with two lines. Moderate emphasis with one line. Perpendicular lines between words denote pauses. Two for a longer pause, one for shorter. With wavy lines the presenter can show upward or downward inflection. Each person can develop his or her own method of notation. Using the word processing program on the computer can provide interesting possibilities. Colored notation can help show emotional content. Have several copies of the script for practicing and developing. Once there is a satisfactory performance script, make a second copy of it in case one is misplaced."

He continues by advising:

"Body language, gestures and facial expressions are included in the concept of animation. For an exercise during a rehearsal, try putting a gesture, action or facial expression with every word. Then cut it back and go for the appropriateness—fitting the animation to the meaning. This experiment can help free up those 'stiff' performers. Practice or rehearse the presentation several times. Use a mirror, a tape recorder and/or a video recorder. Try it on a friend or family member."

While preparing for your reading you need to look ahead to learn as much as you can about what you will face.

"Where is the performance to take place and for whom? Get a clear idea of the stage area for the presentation and of the available lighting. Will there be a lectern or speaker's stand? Will there be a microphone? Is it on a stand, hand held or a lavaliere microphone? Will there be an opportunity for a sound check? Can there be a rehearsal or at least a 'walk through' in the performance space? Who is the intended audience? How many people will there be? How much do they know about haiku? What is the age range? Why are they there? Clear answers to all the above questions are the ideal, but more often there will only be few answers so always be prepared to improvise."

Among his suggestions on what to wear:

"The center of communication is the eyes. Don't obstruct the view of the eyes with hair, a hat, or dark glasses. Keep the chin up. If eye contact with the audience bothers the presenter, then look just above the heads of the audience. Avoid looking down at the floor too much. If the poem requires looking down, then look at a spot on the floor about ten feet ahead."

Professor Cushman even has advice on how to get through those moments of waiting for your turn to perform:

"Before 'taking the stage' a forced yawn can relax the face and jaw muscles, which helps allow for natural facial expression and speech. A few deep breaths will also help. If the script has to be held, press the palms of the hands together in an isometric way for five to eight seconds. This helps to prevent shaking hands. Keep the knees 'soft' and the pelvis gently rolled under to prevent vibrating legs. Quietly hum a favorite song or hymn to loosen the vocal mechanism. Lick the lips and swallow. Smile with the teeth slightly apart. Enter! Break a leg!"

Don't forget that poetry readings are grand opportunities, not only for introducing your haiku to a wider audience, but also for selling your books. If you have not yet published a book of your haiku, it is wise to make a give-away of either a brochure or small booklet of your haiku, with your name on it so they remember you when your big book does come out. Many people enjoy reading haiku more after they have heard them spoken, as they continue to find meaning in them.

If you have books to sell, make arrangements before the reading for another person to take charge of the merchandising. You do not want to be concerned with making change for a twenty while you impress a stranger with the inner mysteries of the haiku form.

The ultimate vocal sharing of your haiku can be done by making a tape or burning a CD. First of all, you need some practice in speaking before a microphone because a mic is not something with which you simply have a conversation like an eyeless friend. This, for most people, is not easy to do, so you need to practice ignoring the microphone, cords, and whirring machinery.

As in a reading before a live audience, you need to have a program for your recording—a tightly organized script of haiku and banter (if any). You can decide if you wish to have a musical accompaniment. Your choice of music will probably depend more on the talents of either you or your friends. Like anything, the music can be an addition or a distraction according to your tastes and abilities. Listen to other recordings of poetry readings to find your ideal and go after it. Don't use copyrighted material borrowed from other media no matter how tempted you may be.

Along the way you may need professional help with sound equipment. It is doubtful you will get rich on the profits of your recording (prove me wrong!), but do it for those who will wish to know you better even when you have left this earth.

Making Copyright Work for You

Before discussing publishing further, let us address the issue of copyright first. Many beginning writers have exaggerated fears of someone stealing their work. They do not realize how strong the desire is in each of us to say what is within us in our very own way. Thus, ninety-nine percent of poets would not even think of signing their name to the work of someone else because they are convinced their work is superior, and since they have so much of their own work in various notebooks and drawers there is no reason to try to publish someone else's poem. Still, a person needs to be aware of the one percent, usually a beginning writer, who steals a poem.

According to my reading of copyright law (I am not a lawyer, and my comments come as a writer and are not legal advice), a work is copyrighted as soon as the author has put it into a retrievable form. This means that simply writing your haiku down on a paper or even speaking it into a recorder, or typing it on a computer, makes it your property. And it remains your property as long as you live, and the property of your heirs for seventy years. At this time, they may renew the copyright if they wish, for another seventy years.

What is important about copyright protection is establishing the date the work was written. In any cases of dispute, you would have to prove that your copy of the work was recorded before the release of the same work by someone else. In the old days, before computers, a method was to make a copy of the poem, article or script, date it, put it into an envelope, and mail it to yourself. Without opening the envelope, (but keep a copy so you can check on what material is sealed away in it), put both in a safe place. Due to the postmark and the authority of the federal government agency, it can be proved that on a certain date you owned this material.

Having your work published in a magazine is also paper proof that you had your name with these words— a good reason to buy and save the magazines in which your poems are published.

With computers this process is even easier. You can type up your work, email it to yourself, print out a paper copy which will automatically put the date on the pages, and save these. If you submit your poem to a users' list, and if they keep an archive, you can use this to establish proof of the date of your copyright.

According to most small magazines in which poetry is published, the work is considered on loan. As long as the magazine is holding accepted work, it is unethical to submit this work elsewhere. As soon as the issue is published, the author regains his or her right to republish the work —this is usually stated as: "all rights return to the author." You can resubmit it elsewhere if the next magazine's policy accepts previously published material. If you sell your work to a magazine, what you are selling is the copyright or the right for them to copy it from your possession.

You do have to watch out for publishers who pay for poems or articles with either cash or in copies of the magazine. This can be construed to mean that you have sold them the copyright to your work, and that if you wish to publish the work elsewhere, you must get their permission each time.

Remember, you cannot copyright a phrase, so if someone steals your favorite phrase, you will have to grin and share it. Also, you cannot copyright just part of a haiku. Changing one word or inverting the line order makes the poem new, and no longer yours.

So what if someone really does publish your poem without your permission, or even worse, as their own poem? A legal process is only viable if you have been cheated out of the money they made with your work or kept you from earning from it. If someone has made money with your poem, you will have a case, especially if you can prove that you had a prior exact copy of the work. But your monetary losses have to be enough to impress a lawyer that s/he can make money defending you. If only your honor and/or ego has been diminished, the best you can do is to approach the editor/publisher and demand a correction—that the poem be accredited to you by being reprinted with your name.

The fear of someone copying your work should not keep you from bringing your work to the public. In fact, you are safer from copyright infringement if you do publish because you will have additional proof that you had made a certain poem public on a specific date.

Getting Your Haiku into Magazines

The traditional place for beginning publication is usually in magazines. But which one? There is a wide assortment of magazines dedicated to the Japanese genres, and the editors of almost all of these would be glad for more subscribers. If you wish to publish, do have the courtesy to first subscribe to the magazine. Or at least obtain a sample copy before you send your work. Study the magazine and think carefully if you would be pleased to see your words printed on these pages—among this group of writers. It is a very individual choice, and the wide variety of magazines proves that each venue is not for everyone. Once you find an editor who accepts your poems, it is easier to branch out to other magazines.

For those needing quicker gratification, there is the World Wide Web. Online poetry magazines abound—just do a search. You have your choice of e-zines (magazines published on the Web), user lists (where you join a group that circulates work among themselves without an editor), or you can make your own Web site. Again, a Web search will show you plenty to think about while planning your own site. The Web lives up to its name in that it is possible to establish connections to other similar sites so that their visitors can also find your site.

But what if the Web is too ethereal for you, and what you want is paper with your poems printed on it—a real book? What are your options?

Getting Your Haiku in Print

What writer does not dream of writing a book? By writing haiku you are closer to having a book of your work printed than by any other form. If you are serious with your work and your abilities, you can, in a fairly short time, have enough haiku together for a book. Whereas one or two haiku may not be very impressive, a whole book of them could surely astonish others with your gifts and potential.

I am not being facetious. I believe that each person can and should write haiku. And I believe that it is possible that the book in each one of us can be a haiku book.

As any publisher will gladly tell you, poetry books from unknown authors do not sell well. Anthologies sell slightly better than poetry books by single authors. Until a few years ago, most publishers, ill-informed and unsure of whether a haiku can even be written in English, stayed as far from the genre as legally possible.

But you do not have to give up; you can make a book of your haiku yourself. Before photocopying became popular, small books of haiku were mimeographed and stapled. Once photocopying could be done on normal paper, there was no reason to pay a printer or be forced to print too many books.

Many persons just want to make a small booklet of their haiku. These little books, perfect for tucking into an envelope to accompany a letter, or adding a personal touch to a gift, serve as a writer's business card and way of introduction to new friends.

Books, consisting of a cover and pages of text, can be

as simple as sheets printed directly from your computer or pages photocopied, and then folded, punched, and hand-tied together. The next step up is to have the center spine of the booklet stapled. If you have only a desk-style stapler, your pages will have to be four inches or less wide so you can reach the center of the spine. The other option is to staple the pages along the left margin. The disadvantage of this is that the pages never conveniently lay open unless the sheet is bent, and it never folds back neatly. The advantage is that you do not need to trim the pages because they are even on all sides.

Many copy centers offer the use or rental of long-necked staplers, so your book width is only determined by the size of stapler they offer. This type of booklet is called "saddle-stapled," meaning the spine, or saddle, is held together with a staple. If you are paying a per-staple price, remember that the book needs at least two staples per copy. Also, one can only put so many folded pages together—the limit is about fifteen or twenty sheets of paper—before the book fans open and will not stay closed.

Even with three or four folded sheets, laid with the folds together, the edges of the sheets will begin to extend on the right margin. Try it with some scraps of paper—and you will see what I mean. One can leave this edge ragged, but the booklet looks much better if the right side of the book is trimmed. An ordinary paper cutter will handle the edge of a few sheets, but if the book has more than that, you will need to take your booklets to a printer to have them trimmed on a blade cutter.

Another binding method is comb binding, which has been popular for cookbooks because this is the only style of bookbinding where the pages lie perfectly flat. Combs, which look like heavy-duty plastic straws with teeth patterns cut in them, can be purchased in many sizes and colors, and cost about twenty-five cents or less, depending on how many and where you buy them. The problem is that you need a fairly expensive machine to punch the little rectangular holes and to hold the combs open in order to insert the pages. Again, you may be able to rent the machine at a copy shop. Some persons feel that the plastic looks cheap, and so there is also a system that uses wires. Depending on the style and feel of your book, this may seem too utilitarian for your haiku, but your ingenuity can make it work for you if you wish.

It is also possible to photocopy the text pages of your book, have a printer print the covers, and then have a bindery professionally put them together. The result will look as good as any paperback on the bookseller's shelves. If you want only two to three hundred copies, this method is certainly one to consider.

If you wish to have more copies than this, you will probably find it more cost-effective to go with lithographing the pages—the normal way of printing a book —instead of photocopying them. And on the subject of printing companies—a good one is worth its weight in gold. Ask around among persons who have recently done a book themselves. They will gladly regale you with their printer stories. Get estimates. If this is your first book, consider paying a bit more to employ a local printer. He or she will probably take the extra time to hold your hand through the steps that the big company, a half-a-continent away, will not be able to do. Know your own level of business savvy. Know or learn how to get an estimate, how to read a contract, and ask questions when in doubt.

If you are going this far, you are basically becoming a publisher yourself. Think of a name for your press, check in the big volumes of *Books in Print* to make sure someone hasn't already had the same brainstorm. For one book you may not need to get a business license, but if you intend to sell very many books, you will need to get a resale license from your local sales tax board. This involves quarterly reports of sales and payments if they think your business is big enough for them to maintain paper work and if you charge sales-tax. If you wish to go in even deeper, you can register your press with R.R. Bowker, 245 West 17th Street, New York, NY 10011, for a fee. Then your company will be given a number and a set of numbers that you can assign to each of your books. This is called an ISBN—an International System Book Number. As you publish future books, you send them advance notice about the book, which they then print in *Books in Print*.

When you get this set up you can apply to the Library of Congress for a Catalog Card Number at Library of Congress, Cataloging in Publication Division, Washington, DC 20540. There is no fee for this, but you are expected to send them two copies of the published book. They pay the postage, however, and keep copies in the Library of Congress.

If all of this is scary stuff to you, once again consider submitting your manuscript to the editor of one of the small literary presses. With them you can avoid the sneer that your book is "self-published," and you will have the advantage of having an ISBN, which you will need to sell your book in stores, as well as a Library of Congress number and card data information. In addition, you will have someone who can advise you on the book, how to do it, and even, if you agree, to edit the material. If you have a publisher, you will have someone else out there managing the printers for you. And you will have someone else to blame for any typographical errors in your book!

There is no thrill like opening a new book and seeing your name in it. And if you are taking yourself seriously as a poet, you need to do whatever it takes to get your work into print. Whether you offer a manuscript to a publisher or do the book yourself, you still need to cull your collection of haiku, organize them, and give your readers your best.

It is very hard to separate oneself from the rush of emotion that either inspired the words or the joy you may have felt upon the creation of your haiku. Letting them cool off by putting them away for a period of time may be enough to let you spot any of the weaknesses. Seeing the haiku after a lapse of time separates the you-as-editor from the you-as-writer far enough for some objectivity to squeeze in. If time and strange fonts do not help enough, there is always the oral test—to see if someone else even understands your haiku.

Organizing Your Haiku for Publication

Traditionally, English haiku books have followed the

ancient Japanese practice of presenting the poems according to the four seasons. Usually beginning with spring, because it is the time of new beginnings, such a scheme gains significance due to the readers' own memories of past years. This method also makes it easier to find a remembered haiku—if it has a strong connection to a season. This method will not work if many of your haiku are about people or lack indications of the season.

You may decide that the haiku are centered around an event (a trip, a spiritual journey, or even a love affair) or a thing (a pet, a hobby, or a person). The need in Westerners to tell a story is so strong that it is fairly easy for us to arrange haiku in a narrative or chronological order. The advantage of this system is that readers too are trained to follow stories, and the inherent desire to see how the tale ends may be just the incentive the reader needs to keep turning pages until the last haiku.

Haiku, like rich chocolates, need to be savored one at a time. Another way of putting some time and space between the haiku is to insert prose pieces between them. It does seem to help to keep a reader involved in a book if the mind can stretch its legs and run with the rapidity of prose between the torque points of the haiku.

Another method of spacing and pacing the haiku in a book is to have illustrations that break up the reader's headlong rush for the next haiku. It is not easy to find an art style that reflects the simplicity and directness of the haiku without either overpowering the words or undermining the meaning. There is a growing interest in combining art and haiku within or without books. The Japanese term is called *haiga* (HI-GAH). Again, this is not new—Bashō left many examples of unpretentious brushstroke drawings to which he added his verse.

Most English writers were not practiced enough with the brush to imitate these *haiga,* but as digital and computer-enhanced photographs have come within the reach of a wider audience, someone got the idea of printing words directly on photographs. Along with the advent of the scanner was the possibility of combining one's haiku with any visual representation, and soon the Internet made it possible for Web sites to show photographs along with haiku.

Other Ways of Publicizing Haiku

Here are some additional ideas of how others have shared their haiku.

1. It has long been a practice, when writing letters among friends, to include a current haiku, either as a date in the beginning or as a closure. If the letter is well written, and the haiku is well chosen, you have a perfect example of a *haibun* (HI-BUN, a literary form combining prose and either a tanka or haiku). In this way, even letter writing can again be a true art form.

2. Haiku is a natural for the art form known as "mail-art" that is still practiced by a small group of artists. Instead of making pictures for a museum, these people use their envelopes as their medium of expression and commit their work and art to the vulgarity of the post office. Rubber stamps have played a part in this art form with carved block-print pictures and haiku. Others

simply write a haiku on the back of the envelope, where it acts as a blessing or prayer for the letter.

3. People who make their own greeting cards have realized that haiku is a natural for this, and even some commercial companies are interested in using haiku for their cards.

4. Some make little booklets of haiku by saving the envelopes from daily mail. These are recycled by folding, punching, and hand-tying them into weird little booklets. The result being a cover and about eight or ten pages. Yes, there is writing and printing on the page, but the trick is to integrate this with the haiku or glue something over it—a stamp or a drawing—so each page is different. Sometimes the haiku is handwritten or makes use of alphabet stamps.

5. Any gift is more personal if a handwritten haiku comes with it. There is also an art to choosing the paper, the ink, and even the scent so that all fit together and elevate the sense of the haiku.

6. Haiku are perfect for T-shirts—just the right amount of reading and worthy of being pondered.

7. Haiku have been written on tea bowls and even commercially on aluminum cans of tea. The Ochi Tea Company in Japan regularly has contests, open to English writers, to choose the haiku for their cans.

8. Haiku go to parties, especially ones held outdoors. It is a tradition in Japan to have a party on the seventh day of the seventh month (called *Tanabata*—TAN-NAH-BAH-TAH) to write haiku on slender paper streamers and to tie them to a bamboo tree.

9. A variation on this is to write a haiku on a piece of

paper and to tie it on a bell as a wind-catcher.

10. Imaginative persons have written their haiku on banners and stood waving them on street corners, as Paul Reps used to do.

11. Australia has adopted the practice from Japan of carving famous haiku on large boulders. These are placed in special places so passersby can walk from haiku to haiku.

12. Ty Hadman once told me that when his daughter was lying ill in a children's hospital, he dressed up in a tuxedo, and tied his haiku to strings attached to a stick with bells on it. He went from room to room jingling and making merry for each of the sick children. As a prize, each child got to pull off a haiku to keep for his or her very own.

Teaching Haiku in Schools

Now, the teachers among the readers of this book may be expecting to read that haiku is a perfect way to start students off on their way to poetry. That is correct, but what is more important than teaching how to write a good haiku is to convey the ideas so that each child learns, understands, and believes that he or she can be a poet. In our society we have become so specialized that it is easy to think that poems are written only by someone else—the professional poet. Poetry should be seen as being used by everyone in the same way that we all hum or sing songs even though we are not pop stars. We learn to sing by singing the songs we learn from listening to others. But the greatest joy in singing is when we make up our own songs. If a teacher can instill the idea in the students, give them this empowerment, and then the knowledge to also write their own poetry, think how much richer their later lives will be. And because haiku is short, and can be as simple as the person wishes to make it, truly anyone capable of speaking can make a haiku.

Because the students may be more familiar with hip-hop and rap songs than haiku, it is helpful to ease them into this all-important beginning. Weeks before haiku comes up in your curriculum, begin writing a haiku every day or so in the upper corner of the blackboard. Leave it there long enough for it to be read several times and pondered. You might consider finding a selection of haiku that reflects the current season. By changing these offered haiku frequently, you are more likely to find one that fits each child's interest. Only when the student's mind becomes a part of a poem will there be the interest in reading more haiku, and then writing it.

You need to be prepared to explain not only how to write a haiku but also how to read it. Sometimes just hearing a haiku read, with inflections and/or gestures, is enough to make the light of realization appear. If not, then telling a story of your understanding of the haiku—putting the images into an extended language—will fill out the unspoken parts of the haiku. Then with a small step and a gentle twist, you can show them how to do this very same thing themselves. You can turn the tables around so that they write as well as they read.

It has been convenient to teach that haiku is a seventeen-syllable poem about nature, but as you have seen, this rule cannot always be applied in English—so drop it. The instruction that can be followed is that suggesting that the haiku contain three lines of short, long, short.

You do not have to limit the beginners to the range of subjects in nature either. Just encourage them to use images they perceive with their senses—hearing, seeing, smelling, tasting and touching—because this is nature, too. Even six to eight words, not in a sentence, can be enough for a haiku. This gives a "can-do" feeling for even the least word-happy student.

Be firm about getting the students to think outside of and beyond themselves. Part of growing up is moving away from the self-centered life of babyhood. A good practice is to work with poetry from outside of the person—and haiku is perfect for this. If the haiku the class are writing is in the manner of "my hat blew off / I chased it / down the street," help them to move the emphasis from themselves to the action they are observing. Put the action in the poem in the present tense and move away from memory with "March winds / rolling down the street / my hat," or something even better.

If some students simply cannot get started, it can be helpful to give them a first line. Most appropriate would be a phrase suitable for the current season: end of summer, falling leaves, first frost, pine tree, snow falling, melting snow, spring rain, daffodil, summer begins. It is always hard to get the first word of a poem down on that empty paper, but by naming an element of the season their minds will already have begun a journey through their own experiences.

If others simply cannot produce anything, you might be prepared to offer them a haiku unknown to them with the last line cut off. Just giving them the beginning two lines could be enough to take them to an experience they may have had and permit them to finish the haiku in their own way. If their line is different from the original one, the poem is considered their own.

Be gentle and accepting of whatever the student writes with honest intent. When students begin to feel comfortable with a method, be firm in encouraging them to try new ways. In your eagerness to keep the students' interest in the form, resist the urge to hold contests or to compare results. Teach them to treasure their experiences and their haiku.

Do display the haiku. Replace your previous haiku selection by writing one of the student's haiku each day on the board and by placing the haiku corner low enough that they can write their own haiku. Seeing the verse in their own handwriting is a powerful connection for students and shows them their own worth and achievement. Think of displaying the haiku in any of the ways listed in the previous section.

Or if the class begins to accumulate enough haiku, teach simple bookmaking. The students can either make individual booklets of their own haiku, or you can make a class project of an anthology so that everyone gets a copy of all the poems.

Using Haiku as Therapy

Sometimes it is easier for a person to reveal his or her emotional climate or perception of the world through a poem than to state it directly or to even know it. Even though haiku are not supposed to discuss the writer's feelings or emotional state, the very fact that the names of the images in the haiku do carry emotional charges that are meaningful to the author will tell the therapist how the patient is perceiving the world around him or her. When diagnosing what the patient may be feeling, one can take a look at the images to see to what things the person is attracted. Any word or phrase that surfaces repeatedly needs to be analyzed for deeper content and meaning.

Beyond its use as a diagnostic tool, haiku has other purposes also. By being cool and detached—concerned with the world around the person—the search for haiku draws the person's mind outside of the internal dialogues. Just getting the inner monologue turned off for minutes at a time is a step in the right direction toward better mental health for anyone.

Again, because the haiku is short, a person can think about what to say and how to say it even while being in situations that would normally cause anxiety. The mental energy which formerly was used in reinforcing the anxiety can be turned around into creating order out of the chaos. The cool, objective stance of haiku offers a relief from an excess of feelings. If the mind is searching for images outside of a person, it is in a place safe from obsessive thoughts. The small activity of writing down a haiku is a vital connection to reality.

Another part of mental health is helping a person to access his or her intuition. As long as the connection between the person and his or her inner world is broken there is no healing. Haiku offers a safe way to begin to visit this sometimes thought-to-be scary part of ourselves.

There is the idea that any creative act puts one in touch with one's Higher Self, God, or the Divine. There are a thousand ways to do this, and haiku is one of them.

Where Can Haiku Take You in the Future?

The short answer is everywhere. Even in America, more and more radio stations are sponsoring a few minutes of reading haiku each day.

In spite of valid gripes about the Internet, it has been a boon for haiku. The proliferation of sites dedicated to haiku shows how many people have a deep love for the form. When you understand the learning, work, and equipment it takes to set and maintain a Web site, you can appreciate how important this aspect of poetry is to a growing number of persons.

In the paper publishing world, various little haiku groups had a tendency to isolate themselves. This was partly due to a strong belief that they alone were right about how to write a haiku and partly the result of the cost to the reader of subscribing to a wider circle of publications. The ease with which someone new to haiku can find a compatible group online with which to share and study haiku is an opportunity so new that it almost makes one giddy.

On one Web site, haiku was used in a lighthearted manner in praise of Spam, a brand of spicy canned pork. The Web site became quite popular and thousands of haiku, or what the purists would call "haiku-like," poems introduced haiku to people who had never heard of it. Many of these Spam haiku used wordplays, puns, and humor—a facet of haiku that is often overlooked by those who think of haiku as poetry or a serious art form.

In addition to the physical realms where haiku is expanding, the form is also undergoing internal changes as it moves into different countries, cultures, and languages. One cannot bottle up haiku and attempt to keep it pristine, shaped by only one precept. That would cause the form to wither and die. As long as persons are stretching it, pulling it this way and that, making the genre fit their visions, it will remain alive. It is a joy to realize that each and every person who works at the form has a hand in changing its shape.

The next step for haiku is for it to be so integrated into poetry that the form is taught not only at the grade school level but also in colleges and universities. Only when haiku becomes an accepted form for the work of professional poets will it overcome its present stigma and truly be able to take English poetry to the next step. The process is happening all around us—that is what makes it so hard for us to see the progress. Each person who now takes up haiku as a serious poetry form is part of the future of haiku.

Four

USING YOUR HAIKU SKILLS IN RELATED POETRY FORMS

A Concise History of Oriental Poetry

The beginnings of poetry are mostly lost in the misty breath of oral history. Poetry then and now was "saying things"—pronouncing with human breath the magic names of things and even beings designed by the minds and hearts of ancestors. These incantations or songs to gods were later organized to become a part of religion.

It was only a small step, but a huge change, to move from petitioning the favors of the gods through the declarations of love to expressions of desire for a person with the purpose of petitioning other kinds of favors. When politicians saw the power and control the common people gave to the singers of religion, they began to use poets to laud, and record in an oral tradition, their own battles and good deeds. One could probably say this was the beginning of campaign advertising.

Poetry is a social function. We usually learn our poetry from someone else. Thus, the earliest Japanese poetry was in imitation of Chinese forms. But since poetry cannot be duplicated exactly, each culture changes the form to some degree to make it its very own. In Japanese, the quatrains of Chinese settled into a five-part poem first named *uta* (OU-TAH, "song"), then *waka* (WAH-KAH, "a Japanese poem"), and finally *tanka* (TAHN-KAH, "a short poem or elegance").

Because Chinese poetry was built on parallelism there were two parts to the tanka form. They were given the names of *kami no ku* (KAH-ME NO COO) and *shimo no ku* (SHE-MO NO COO). The kami no ku, the upper verse, consisted of the first three units, what we now think of as lines, and the lower verse pivoted or twisted away with additional meaning in the last two-line section.

The popularity of this form reigned supreme from the earliest recorded Japanese poetry, for almost six hundred years, and is yet today an important genre in modern Japanese poetry. When the tanka was replaced by the *renga* (WREN-GAH, "linked elegance or poem"), these two parts of the tanka were simply shifted from one author to two. When two persons wrote a tanka, it was called a *tan renga* (TAN WREN-GAH, "short linked elegance"). It was again a small but vital step for tan renga to be linked by additional stanzas or authors to become a renga.

Renga, which started as a game after tanka contests, became so much fun and enlivened the poetry scene so greatly that the genre was slowly tamed and renamed. The original fun and games version of renga, which was called *mushin* (MOO-SHIN) renga, was relegated to be only party entertainment. The more serious, artistic form of the genre was called *ushin* (OU-SHIN) renga and was soon given complex rules and the impressive regulations of an official state poetry. There were about three centuries in Japan when this serious poetic renga was far more popular than waka/tanka. In this bloom of attention, and with an increasing addition of rules, the differences between the two kinds of renga form began to widen. The result of overwhelming rules and guidelines was the strangulation of innovation and popularity.

In rebellion against the strictness of the serious form of renga, poets revived the mushin or comical form. Part of the interest in this older form was political. The system of emperors had been disempowered, and now military factions held the ruling positions. Because the poetical renga was closely connected with and fostered by the emperor, the shoguns, or military class, wanted to have their own kind of renga without the associations to the imperial court.

The military class lacked the training in literature routinely given to the members of the emperor's court, so in order to write renga, even in the easier form, they had to have schools, and these schools had to have teachers.

Because the government was a military regime, each of the provinces had to have members of this class, called *daimyo*, or warlords, reinforced with the samurai, warrior class, stationed in all the outposts. As part of their meetings, and aside from the business of ruling, was the pleasure and the feeling of culture that was fostered by writing renga together. The farther from the seat of government, then in Kamakura, the less educated was the outpost commander and the more pressing was the need for a teacher. Thus came into being a system of renga masters who traveled from place to place teaching and instructing while leading parties where poetry was written.

Though it must have been a thrill to be the honored

guest of an often wealthy government official or merchant, travel in seventeenth century Japan was by foot or horseback through wild regions still controlled by bandits. For such teachers it took considerable social skills, not to mention the possibility of political intrigue, to step lively and look good.

It was the custom that the renga master was given the honor of writing the first link to the renga. It was the uniqueness of this first link, then called a *hokku*, that made the next step in Japanese poetry. This verse, as no other in the renga, could be thought up without having to take into account a previous stanza. This meant that the wise renga master could, in his idle moments, write a variety of hokku, tuck them up his sleeve, and pick the the one most appropriate to the situation when starting the next renga.

Enter Bashō. In spite of what you may have read, Bashō was neither a haiku master nor a writer. He was a renga master. He was one of those men traveling around to teach others by guiding them through the riffles and pitfalls of renga writing. As his renga school followed him wherever he was, his students were not gathered in one place. Thus it became necessary to get them all on the same page by making a book of collected hokku that he approved of as being worthy of a renga. This book was called, in a typically humble manner, *A Bag of Charcoal*.

You may be thinking that this is the beginning of haiku books, but it took two intervening centuries to get to this point. At the end of the 1800s there lived in Matsuyama a journalist named Masaoka Shiki. When he became incapacitated with tuberculosis of the spine, he switched from journalism to poetry and poetic criticism. Due to his prior connection to newspapers, he was quickly able to get his new ideas out to a wide, accepting audience.

Following his death, Bashō had been elevated to the god-like level of a national hero. Many, many books were written about Bashō, his verses and his commentary, and even places he had visited became famous—and still are. However, Shiki found this worship of Bashō and his work quite repugnant. So he pulled out an old, trusty political ploy, used by lesser poets before him. He coined a new word for the work of Bashō. Whereas Bashō called the beginning link of a renga a *hokku* (HOKE-COO) and the internal links of a renga the *haikai* (HI-KI), Shiki combined the *hai* of haikai with the *ku* of hokku to come up with the word we now use—haiku.

When the French first began translating these short verses from Japanese, they used the proper word—hokku—because they were still called that in Japan. But when later translations were made, the term haiku had been adopted by the Japanese for the genre, so that now we are stuck with having two words for nearly the same thing. We still reserve the use of the words hokku and haikai for the stanzas of a renga, but any haiku could also be called a hokku or haikai.

Now that you have an overview of these poetry forms, let's take a closer look at each of them to see how to write them.

Tanka: The Modern Centuries-old Genre

Nearly everything you have learned about writing haiku applies to writing tanka. So if you have gotten this far, you only need to make a few adjustments in goals and techniques. Some persons, in introducing the tanka form, give the impression that one only needs to add the author's feelings to a haiku. Yes, it is possible to write a tanka by doing that, but tanka is much more than an expression of a person's feelings. It is the search for relationships between ourselves and our world.

First of all, it might be helpful to recall that tanka was the poetic form used, advanced, and admired by the imperial court. It was the genre of professional poets, the highborn, and, like it or not, was often done best by women. Thus the form was more lyrical, refined, and more emotional.

If you have written some haiku, you have written, more or less, half a tanka. A beginning exercise in learning to write tanka is to take one of your haiku and practice adding two more lines to it. If you are counting syllables, these two additional lines would consist of seven syllables each. If you are working with short, long, short line shapes, just make the additions, if you can, about as long as the second line.

If you decide to write a form genre, then make an effort to keep the form recognizable in your final product. Following a form will force you to bend your mind in ways that freely jotting the first thing that comes to mind will not. It is the exercise of making your ideas fit into a form that forces you to stay with the poem longer and to think more deeply about what you are trying to say. As it is when you learn to dance, you follow the examples until your body and mind know so well what to do you can trust your own inner being to do the poem/dance well.

The extra material in tanka has a couple of very important jobs to do. It is not as if you can just glue two haiku together to get a tanka. Within the tanka there is a switch of time, place, person, thing, or voice in order to create a leap or define a new relationship. These factors are so important; let us look at them individually.

1. A change in time means that if one part of the verse is set in the past (no longer are you constrained to write only in the present tense as in haiku), the other section can be set in another time frame—either the present or the future. This allows tanka to move the reader backwards and forwards in time, which expands the possibilities so much that the haiku seems absolutely oppressive.

> last day of school
> we carry our shoes home
> in our lunchboxes
> the next day crayon containers
> now a granddaughter's antique

2. Because tanka allows the author to play with time, it also allows one to move out of reality into fantasy, imagination, and other thought processes. In tanka one is not bound by just what is, but is open to the emotional life of the author. By being able to switch times, the author can work with memories, and memories are always loaded with emotion, so this fits the genre perfectly.

> too old for new love
> the moon rises each night
> as I remember
> the backseats of strange cars
> its helpful light afterwards

3. A change in place also enlarges the scene of the poem exponentially. The above tanka also has a change of place—the moon in a woman's adult life and in the backseats of cars when she was younger.

4. A change in person actually means you can switch persona within the poem. Part of the poem can read as if one person does or thinks one thing, and in the next section, another person has a different opinion or action. Even in such a short form, this fosters optimum exhilaration. If half of the tanka is framed in the cool, detached language of a haiku, you can, by writing of your own opinions in the second part, make this classical move.

> in seven years
> the body replaces itself
> how is it
> I know in every cell
> the hour we first met

5. A change in voice can be shown by a switching from one group of people to another or by having a change in verb tense or going from the singular to the plural.

pieces of people
not speaking to each other
on the beach
we find a strange pink glob
the tongue of a drowned man

6. A change in things which are related is a technique
   that works very much like associations and compar-
   isons of things in haiku.

as your finger
enters the sticky flap
of the envelope
how I wish my letter
to you was me

7. The change can be shown in parallels between situa-
   tions and things. This is the most common device of
   tanka.

reading the will
she was so careful
yet so little left
even her houseplants
have lost their leaves

8. There can also be parallels between human feelings
   and things so that in the action of the thing is revealed
   the author's emotional state.

your letter
left me at sea to know
where we are going
puzzled the paper folded
a boat set adrift

9. There can be parallel movements between things rising and other things falling, which can tie together dissimilar things or actions in the two sections.

a wet road
flowing into sky at the top
of the hill
twin lights appear to descend
a friend is coming to visit

10. The use of a shared adjective or verb is another way of tying together the two parts of a tanka. "Faded" describes both the shirts and features of the woman. The verb "fit" uses both senses of meaning to "be the right size" and "to associate."

I love
my T-shirts faded
they fit
my graying hair
dimming eyesight

How you make these moves between the two sections of a tanka becomes pivotal. Literally. The most tanka-like aspect of a tanka is creating and using a pivot. When you have mastered this technique, you can do almost anything in the form and still legally call it a tanka. So how to pivot?

If you will, remember again that the very oldest poetical technique is parallelism. Tanka takes the simple device of parallels and stretches the two parts of it so far apart that the reader needs a bridge to get from one idea to the other. The bridge the author creates is the phrase called the pivot.

Look at the middle line of each of the example tanka above. In all of these, the pivot comes in the middle line in the classical manner. Notice how sharing a similar aspect, as stated in the middle, allows the sense to shift back and forth between the two parts. One test of the effectiveness of this technique is to cover the bottom two lines to see if the top three read as a unit with one meaning. If you then cover the top two lines, reusing the third line, this unit gives the pivot phrase another meaning. Do you see how haiku-like the top three lines read and how the mood changes in the bottom half, and yet both share one aspect?

It is considered an advancement to integrate the pivot in the sense of the lines instead of positioning it in the obvious place—the middle line.

> only shopping
> school clothes for the kids
> yet the desire
> to meet him in the mall
> just one glance above the goods

If one had to indicate the pivot of the above, it would be in the first line: the woman is shopping for clothes for her children and wants to be at the same time shopping around for a lover.

By using parallelism the tanka poet is able to write about things which do not yet have names. Poetry is the act of giving names to the nameless. Your first thought may be that there is a word for everything, but think again. Look inside yourself at your own feelings. Is there any word that exactly explains how you feel at this moment? You may be able to think of a general term but does that alone adequately express you and your individual expression of an emotion? How could you tell someone else exactly how you are feeling when there is no precise word that describes it? This has been the challenge of poets through the ages since humans learned to speak. The answer is parallelism. You find some aspect of the world of nature that looks or seems like your feeling. Even non-poets use this technique so easily that you may not even be aware that it is a poetic process.

Another term for parallel thinking is *simile*. Similes are so common, yet so exact that they have come to be an integral part of the folk knowledge of any culture's language. The technique is to reveal, through a comparison of two dissimilar things, how one unnameable thing can be defined through the image of the known. Like a hit on the head, the idea is as clear as glass.

A metaphor is much like a simile with the signposts of "like" and "as" removed. Thus, it is one step up in difficulty in creating and in understanding. Metaphors are also called tropes or figurative expressions of speech. Metaphor is the most basic tool of the poet and deserves a deeper study than is given here.

Ah, you wish an example of a metaphor? Homer's phrases are perhaps the most famous: "the wine-dark sea" and "rosy-fingered dawn." You see how he simply took the idea that "the sea was as dark as wine" and "the dawn sky looked as if it has rosy fingers reaching upward," and compacted the words to let the recipient of his words untangle and find the transaction he has made between them and things. As you can imagine, any poetic tool still around since Homer's age is pretty well-worn around the edges. This is why Westerners are so excited about the new-to-them way metaphor is handled in the Orient.

Instead of mashing the two dissimilar elements together in the quickness of a hyphenated phrase, we find that the Japanese simply set each image quietly in its own element but place them side by side (or as poetic critics call it—in juxtaposition). To discover the metaphor in Japanese poetry takes a bit more thinking, knowledge of the culture, and pure joy in discovery—often a reason Westerners find tanka translations "flat." The Japanese are better trained to be subtle, and their poetry works with this aspect to a most refined degree. But because they leave more space between the images, both in actual space on a line and in the distance between the relationships of the images, there is much more room for the readers' minds to explore.

In such short poetry forms, the author and the reader need all the help they can get to enlarge the meanings and associations. The Japanese use a technique they call *honkadori* (HON-KAH-DOE-REE), which we still need to develop in our English tanka. Honkadori can be defined as literary association. This can be as obvious as using a quote from a prior work, or simply referring to a place or character or idea known because of a famous work. Since the success of the use of an allusion implies a knowledge of the literary heritage, it can be used as a secret language, especially when shared between lovers. It is also used as a flaunting of education. The device can be a bridge between a famous poet and a not-yet or hope-to-be famous poet or an act of homage. An honest use of the technique comes when one truly admires the words of another and finds them so outstanding that they should be preserved again in a new poem. In English poetry it is the practice to place such a quote beneath the poem's title and before the first line, but the Japanese offer an example of how to integrate such a homage within the poem itself.

An example of how sensitively this facet can be handled starts with a tanka written by the priest-poet Saigyō in the twelfth century. While on a journey to northern Japan he stopped to rest and wrote this poem:

> Beside the roadway
> a flowing of clear water
> in a willow's shade
> I thought for just a short while
> to linger and take a rest.*

When Bashō visited the same place, and supposedly the same tree, he wrote:

---

* Saigyō, translated by Yuki Sawa and Edith Shiffert in *Haiku Master Buson*. Compton, CA: Heian International, p. 26.

A flooded rice field
now its planting is done I leave –
the willow tree.*

When, fifty years later, Buson visited the same spot,†
now even more famous than before, he wrote this poem:

The willow leaves fall
and the clear water has gone
stones lie everywhere.‡

From these three samples you can see how subjective
the original tanka was, how Bashō's haiku makes a step
away in being a bit cooler and remote—only the willow
tree is shared by both poems. Then see how Buson's
poem, which even though it holds a great deal of sadness,
is even more objective and closely connected to Saigyō's
poem.

For some persons, the opportunity of being able to
express emotions or opinions in tanka is a distinct advan-
tage over the cooler objective style of haiku. Our literary
heritage is much closer to tanka than to haiku. And
therein lies a problem. The initial contact with haiku was
like a sip of clean, cold water after the rich meals of Eu-
ropean poetry. To now offer a haiku-related form that
again allows us to wallow in our feelings could invite us
to fall back into previous excesses. As a culture that

---

* Bashō, ibid.
† It is still possible to see a willow tree in this place, and there is a box
where passersby can put their poems, continuing this connection to ages
past, poetry, and fellow travelers.
‡ Buson, ibid, p. 27.

"wears its heart on its sleeve" and is sometimes referred to as "the me generation," there is a danger that our tanka could become cheapened if they are simply a lamenting or bitching genre of "oh poor me—nobody loves me—how hard my life is."

However, if we adopt tanka as a gift to our loves, the genre can carry, and carry beautifully, heartfelt sentiment. Tanka, historically, was used as a form of communication between lovers, and it seems that this use asks us to continue it. This does not mean that in order to write tanka, the writer needs to start an affair nor confine tanka to this one subject. You can simply rediscover and re-experience the many loves which already surround you in all areas of living. Again, assuming the tanka writer is also working on his or her spiritual advancement, what higher goal is there than to learn to love?

Renga for Writers Who Leap

Everything you have learned so far about haiku and tanka you will need and can put to use for renga. These two genres have taught you how to dance, and now you are ready to glide across the paper in the arms of a stranger. Since there is no sound of music to guide the two of you, the genre offers you a form to follow to keep you in step, to exercise all your skills, and to make it fun to watch you with admiration for your expertise.

Renga is called a collaborative poetry because, generally, two or more persons contribute to the poem. Occasionally renga are written by groups at what is often called a renga party—which has echoes of the times of

Bashō. For these events one person is designated as renga master. He or she is in charge of calling out the season or subject for the next link and decides whether an offered link is good enough to be included in the poem. Another person is appointed as scribe and writes down the accepted links along with the author's name.

The master starts out by asking the most honored guest of the gathering to submit the hokku or three-line beginning stanza. Everyone waits in a respectful silence while this person composes his or her verse. When it is ready, it is spoken aloud to the whole group. This verse is so important for assuring that the renga gets a proper and good beginning that I have seen masters tell the honored guest to "please try again." At one party I attended the poor honored guest spent a half hour trying to come up with the opening stanza. It is no wonder that the wise come to renga parties with some spare verses tucked away in a handy place.

As soon as the hokku, and thus the title of the renga, is established, anyone in the group can offer the next link by speaking the verse aloud. The master listens and will then accept or reject the offering. If nothing offered is pleasing the master, he or she may work with an author on a flawed link to make it adequate. Sometimes others in the group may make suggestions, which the author or the master may or may not accept. Though this may seem a bit painful, especially for shy persons, it is a very productive way of teaching the rules of renga to a group.

Outside of Japan, because persons interested in renga were so rarely in one place together, it became popular for the renga to be written by only two persons, or occasionally three persons. Because of the distance between the partners' homes, the renga had to be sent back and forth through the mail. This slow and laborious method was used by over ninety-five percent of the renga written before the advent of e-mail. Not only does e-mail allow almost instant response, it is possible for the partners to record their comments, thoughts, and ideas alongside the renga as they write the poem.

The computer, aside from e-mail, has also brought together groups to write renga via chat rooms and now "on the fly" with programs such as Ann Cantalow's Poetry Invention, which allows real-time linking.

There is, in Japanese history and today's literature, the solo renga—written by one person. No matter how well done, the solo renga always lacks the tension in the play of emotions that manifests when there are partners. Another form is the book renga, in which haiku or links from another renga are picked out and used for the new responses being written. This method is slightly more advanced because the writer must make the sense of the links fit both the previous and the following link.

Renga is a very unusual genre—very foreign to our way of perceiving literature. We Westerners seem to be bound to wanting and using the narrative as a basic literary structure. Perhaps this is why it is not easy for many poets to appreciate renga, although more modern literature is coming to use its unique contributions.

Renga do not tell a story, nor are the links bound by a theme (usually) or any one set method of choosing subject matter. Renga do not lead the reader to any conclusion or provide answers. In many ways a renga is like overhearing conversation at a dinner party. Each link contributes to the whole poem by relating only to the material given in the directly preceding link. The subject matter of earlier links is carefully avoided so that the reader can never settle down into a comfortable knowledge of what is coming ahead.

The actual worth of a renga is not in the individual links, but in whatever happens in the silent space between the links. Renga is, if anything, the art of transition—how to leap from here to there. Thus, the greatest value or benefit from reading a renga comes from the reader's mind as he or she makes a completely personal journey from link to link. Because each link is written in response to the previous one, and since there are many ways of making these subtle connections, the trained reader of renga observes how the partners solve the problems set up by the rules of the form.

Until Bashō's time, most renga had either one hundred, one thousand, or ten thousand links. Considering the time and effort it took Bashō to get to the place for a renga party, and thinking of how uncomfortable this old hermit might have felt living amongst strangers for an extended period of time, it is no wonder that he devised a renga form using only thirty-six links called the *kasen* (KAH-SEN(d), "poetic sages")—supposedly to honor the thirty-six immortal poets of Japan.

Because the English introduction to renga came from the work of Bashō, we first learned only to write in the thirty-six-link form. Because Bashō made little booklets out of the papers the renga were recorded on—basically two double-sided sheets of paper folded in half and tied together at the crease to make four pages—he decided that the shape of the poem should have six links on the first right-hand page; twelve links on each of the facing pages two and three; and six links on the last page. Sensitive even to the interruption of the turning of the page, it became traditional that the last person to write a link on the page (links numbered 6, 18, 30) also wrote the first link on the next page so that there was a continuation of voice over the change of sheets.

This was a marvelous invention because, if only two persons were writing a renga, it allowed them to switch places. The writer of the three-line stanza, after the turn of a page, was now writing the two-liners. By changing back and forth, no one was leading and no one was following. Only a couple of English writers ignore this switch and keep their respective places throughout the poem.

The other formal feature of the kasen form was the rule that a verse using the moon had to appear on the first three pages and that twice within the poem should be a flower verse. The position of these required links came to have the moon verses at links numbered five, fourteen, and twenty-nine. Flowers, or more specifically cherry blossoms, should be the subject in links numbered seventeen and thirty-five.

Because Bashō wrote these renga at parties, the tone of the stanzas actually followed the rhythm of a social gathering. The first link, or hokku, should refer to the season in which the renga was started. If possible, it should compliment the host and/or give a hint of why this group had gathered. Proper renga to this day, even when done between two people, open with a veiled compliment to the partner.

The response in the second link (*wakiku*, WAH-KEY-COO) should be as polite and gentle, and stay within the same season while acting as an elaboration. This verse must end with a noun.

The third link (*daisan*, DIE-SAN), makes the first gentle side step into a new subject. By ending this link with a verb—usually in English it is a gerund (using an "ing")—the action, though shifted, continues to move on into the rest of the renga.

Throughout the whole first page, all six links should be very slow—meaning the action moves gently from one scene to another, from one idea to another. This is in perfect imitation of the event of going to a stranger's home for dinner. Before sitting down to the meal, you make polite conversation as you attempt to get to know one another.

On the second page, at link #7, the conversation begins to warm up after the first glass of wine. Subjects not allowed on the first page—love, death, religion, and violence—are possible in the twenty-four verses of these facing pages.

The last page, or links #30 on to 36, have a tempo much like the feeling at the end of an evening when the guests are putting on their coats, gathering up belongings, and making farewells. Often the connections are looser, in the same way that at this time of the evening we stop responding to each other as we make plans to meet again, remind someone to call, or say something we almost forgot. The renga should always end on a positive, hopeful note and have some connection to the very first link.

How does one make these connections between links that are so necessary to renga? Kyūsei, a co-editor of the *Tsukuba Shū**—twenty volumes of renga and renga lessons—listed fifteen methods. For you to study these maneuvers, here is a renga Werner Reichhold and I wrote with Bashō. By collecting and translating links written by Bashō in several of his renga, we were able to make him the third partner in this poem written on a hot day in the summer of 1990.

---

* This work, published in 1375, had one volume dedicated to hokku verses alone. The printed history of what later became haiku can be traced to this event.

OLD JOKES WITH ME
Matsuo Bashō
Jane Reichhold
Werner Reichhold

1   **it's so rotten**
no other dogs enjoy
old jokes with me

2   *pass the wine*
raise our spirits

3   always a link
up his sleeves
the brush wets

4   **leather socks get dirty**
walking a muddy path

5   *somebody's missing*
quick put the moon in
a puddle

6   shy eyes
far-out composing

7   spinning down
when does it get
to the bottom?

8   **so the villagers
      laugh at me**

9   *sleeping outdoors
      with friends
      summer constellations*

10   a hand drumming
      pulsates with the sun

11   **a woodthrush manifests
      "as power-spirit I come"
      and cries and cries and cries**

12   *breath wind in mists
      a trail through the maze*

13   meadow walk
      eventually hiding
      a snake

14   **greeting the traveler
      a lamp on the floor**

15   *curving her breast
      the early moon
      very hot*

16   impatient call:
      "Where can we meet?"

17   **sandals in petals**
        yet he's so poor
        his hat's a sack

18   *squint-eyed bag lady*
        famous in New Jersey

19   *picture postcard*
        the come hither look
        of the naked beauty

20   expanded body freedom
        designed for partnership

21   *cats in love*
        satisfied at dawn
        he explains

22   **"I'm collecting songs**
        for the Flax–Reaping Anthology."

23   bundles
        the hand ties with a string
                words

24   *college sonnets saved*
        in a hope chest

25   **more than dreams**
        the real butterfly
        touches one

26   stem after it
        leaves erect

27   *without friends*
        he moves
        to help himself

28   **among that kind**
        the tall pilgrim stands out

29   relief comes
        first light
        on a cedar tip

30   *to an incense stick*
        he also bows

31   *worship service*
        begins as invocation
        crickets chanting

32   **it's so hot it's so hot –**
        the same voice at every gate

33   wet lips
        summer-shine
        opens

34   *snow-clogged mountain pass*
        so steep everyone sweats

35   resting
              the hiker hears
           a wave of color

36   **sunset on a spring lake**
pleasure brings home a poem

Here is a list of the linking techniques as exemplified in the renga "Old Jokes with Me."

1. A very close connection. This is good to use on the first page, as we do in the first two stanzas. Bashō is grumbling that he is lonely because all his old pals are gone—a rather typical lament of someone partially drunk. The answer in this situation is to drink a little more, as is the logical advice in the next link.
2. Contrasting directions. If one verse has as its subject a descending object, as in falling rain, the response can build on an image of rising. In this renga the device is used at link #29—"relief comes / first light / on a cedar tip"—where the light rises up to touch the tip of the tree. Then the answering link—"to an incense stick / he also bows"—has the subject bending down.
3. Contrasting conditions. The dryness of link #32— "it's so hot it's so hot— / the same voice at every gate" —is set against the moistness of the response, "wet lips / summer-shine / opens." Other contrasting conditions are: chaotic-calm; noisy-quiet; exciting-peaceful; night-day; hot-cold, etc.
4. Contrasting sizes. In the ninth link, the "summer

constellations" are contrasted, and yet related to the "sun" in the next link.

5. Associations by cliché. The shamanic drumming of #10 manifests in the power-spirit of #11, which is just outside the bounds of most reality.

6. Associations in literature or allusions to famous texts. Bashō uses this device in link #22, where he makes a small joke between reaping flax (by tying the bundles together) and creating an anthology.

7. Associations in space. The snake in the grass in #13 becomes a lamp on the floor in #14.

8. Associations with usage. The incense stick in #30 and the invocation in #31 are both parts of a religious service.

9. Associations with fame, history, or custom. When Werner asks in link #16, "Where can we meet?" Bashō responds with the most romantic place for Japanese lovers to meet—under cherry blossoms—while at the same time getting in the flower verse.

10. Fragrance. This was a term Bashō used to name the mere hint of the overtones in one link that could be responded to in the next one. Often this technique hinges on the emotional response from one link to another. The control of changing emotions within a renga is an important part of its total construction. One does not want all verses to be happy, nor to be depressingly sad or upsetting, and a great many of them should be like the moments of a day—mostly beige-neutral. But in the same way we need many ordinary moments, each one is necessary for the next one and for the whole. The "expanded body freedom

/ designed for partnership" in link #20 is explained by link #21, "cats in love."

11. Wordplay. It is acceptable and admired to make puns on the words in your partner's link. Here, the "puddle" of #5 is seen as "shy eyes" in #6.

12. Wordplay based on the names of places. This device is often used near the end of the renga to jazz up the language and pull the poem out of too much nature-nature. Here it occurs at #18. In reference to Bashō's "his hat is a sack" is the "new jersey."

Go back and read the renga once more, noticing how often the third line of a link, when read with the two lines of the following link, forms what looks very much like a haiku. It is this kind of closeness that keeps the renga from falling apart, and it is a good thing to check when you've finished your renga.

The list of do's and don'ts for writing a renga can seem endless and some appear extremely arbitrary. However, a student of renga needs to know them.

1. First and foremost, always refer to, or link with, only the immediately preceding verse and not to any of the previous verses. Once a subject has been used, move on to something else or another aspect of it.

2. The first link, or hokku, must be written in the present tense, have an indication of the season, and make some reference, either to the reason for doing the renga or homage to the other partner, in a polite and kindly way. Just any old haiku from your notebook will not be good enough, no matter how good you

think it is. The hokku has to be very special and fulfill its obligations in this place of honor.

3. If there is a string of several either close or distant associations, change the pace by doing the opposite.

4. Do not repeat the same nouns or verbs on a page. Check for this and replace them with synonyms.

5. Don't use too many references to the same sort of things. You'd be surprised how many people get into ruts mentioning water over and over with rivers, ponds, streams, lakes, dew, and even saliva. Other persons get stuck on plants with too many trees, grasses, and flowers.

6. Do not have too many nature links in a row. Mix them up with links about humans; even spots of intellectual thinking or philosophy used judicially can be interesting.

7. Save your moon and flower verses for the links where they belong. If you wish to bring the moon in early, have it not be a full moon but a crescent or new moon. If you are a master, you can occasionally slip up and it is considered diversity. If you are a beginner, it may be considered a fault.

8. All moon verses are considered to be a subject of autumn. If you wish to have your moon in another season, you must label it "winter moon" or "spring moon." The mention of the moon assumes it is full because this is the state in which it is deemed most picturesque.

9. Do not stay within one verb tense. You know haiku should be written in the present tense, but tanka and renga allow you to explore both the past and the future.

Watch for this in the renga. If several verses are written in the present tense, make a change with your link.

10. Do not stay within just one voice. Occasionally speak directly by using the "you" form of address. Also, you can use quotations from others to change from the simple observation mode as in haiku. Even the messages from, say, roadside signs or literary sources are welcomed as variation.

11. If you are not following one of the form sheets with the season and other subjects indicated, remember that spring and autumn links should come in runs of three to five links, and the winter and summer groups should consist of two to three links.

12. Some typical Japanese rules are that insects should be mentioned only once in one hundred verses, dreams only once in a renga, and you should never use the word "woman."

Tan Renga for Short Leaps

The idea of starting to work on a renga with a stranger may be somewhat intimidating, but help is readily available. Before there was renga with many links there was the renga form of only two parts. It is basically a tanka written by two persons. It looks like a tanka, acts like a tanka, but if it takes two persons to write it, the form is called a *tan renga*—"short linked elegance." Tan renga can either begin with the three-part stanza or the two-part stanza. A nice way of complimenting someone who sends you a haiku is to respond with your link to make a tan renga.

old master
weighing air
spills some

– Bambi Walker

Zen students laugh
swallow it whole

– Jane Reichhold

Practice Sheets for Renga Partners

If you are feeling that there is no way you could remember all these rules about renga, there is even more help. By writing a renga on a sheet where the links are numbered, with indication of whose turn it is, along with hints as to what comes next, the partners can concentrate on writing instead of reminding each other of missed rules. Here is a sample form indicating the most basic rules for a renga, which you can copy. This one is set up for two people, but it is easy to change for several partners. If you wish to have copies of the more complicated forms designed for each of the seasons as based on Bashō's examples, they are available online (http://www.ahapoetry.com/rengfmsp.htm). After your renga is written, you can delete all the information in the brackets to make it seem that you understood everything perfectly.

Traditional Kasen Renga
[title—often taken from the first link]
Between:
a – [guest's name]
b – [host's name]

Started:
Finished:

1. [the guest (a) writes 3 lines *hokku*]
2. [the host (b) writes 2 lines *wakiku*]
3. [a – 3 the *daisen* verse should end with a verb]
4. [b – 2]
5. [a – 3. Moon verse.]
6. [b – 2. You should also write #7.]
7. [b – 3]
8. [a – 2]
9. [b – 3]
10. [a – 2]
11. [b – 3]
12. [a – 2]
13. [b – 3]
14. [a – 2. Moon verse.]
15. [b – 3]
16. [a – 2]
17. [b – 3. Flower verse.]
18. [a – 2. You should also write #19.]
19. [a – 3]
20. [b – 2]
21. [a – 3]
22. [b – 2]
23. [a – 3]
24. [b – 2]
25. [a – 3]
26. [b – 2]
27. [a – 3]
28. [b – 2]
29. [a – 3. Moon verse.]
30. [b – 2. You should also write #31.]
31. [b – 3]
32. [a – 2]
33. [b – 3]
34. [a – 2]
35. [b – 3. Flower verse.]
36. [a – 2 *ageku*/closure]

[Copyright © Jane Reichhold 1989. Permission to copy.]

Here are a few guidelines helpful to observe while doing renga with one or more partners by mail. When renga are done at a party, there is usually a renga master to set the guidelines, but when the partners work individually, and more democratically, there needs to be a system of agreement from the beginning.

1. Start with a clear idea of what you intend to write. Will you be doing a traditional kasen renga or a less demanding form? Will you do all thirty-six links or only a *han* (half) renga consisting of eighteen links? Will you be trying an experiment? Whose rules will you be following?
2. Usually the one who wants to do a renga, the host, asks the guest to write the first link. Unless it is otherwise agreed, the host takes care of the renga by making copies, offering it for publication, and keeping the partner(s) informed.
3. Unless someone makes such a terrible error that there is no way you can respond with a link, leave glitches, repeats, and nonsense until the whole poem is written. One writes renga with emotion, and if pointing out corrections and errors angers one of the partners, the lines will become brittle and snappish, and perhaps the renga will be broken off.
4. Send your responses back as quickly as possible. Nothing wrinkles a renga like letting it get old on your piled-up desk. Remember you are working on a living thing.
5. When the poem is complete, allow the first guest to make any corrections in his or her own links that are

necessary. Don't completely replace a link with another one that is very different. If you do, the partner will have to rewrite his or her link and then you will have to rewrite the one following . . . you get the idea. Revise and make minor corrections but don't change out the complete sense of your stanza unless it fits appropriately with the next link.

6. On this corrected version of the renga the host makes corrections to his or her work.

7. Then there can be an exchange of questions about why such and such was done or if the other person really wishes for a certain link to stand as it is. Be courteous, cautious, and polite. You are still clinched cheek to cheek in a dance.

8. By doing a renga it is agreed that either partner may publish the final poem. It is very bad form to do a renga and then withdraw your own links from the work.

Enlarging Anything with Sequences

Now that you understand the renga, let us take the next logical step. You have seen how the tiny units of haiku can be combined in a complicated process to make a longer poem, so perhaps now it is easier to think about writing a sequence.

In our Western literary heritage we are used to having long poems, called sequences, that spin out a thread of thinking over many pages and often lead to a certain conclusion. Sometimes haiku sequences will almost happen in the writing down of many verses during one certain experience. If the haiku are arranged in a sequential order, the form is called a sequence. This order is either built on narrative (the way you would tell a story) or chronologically (the way the events fit together in the order of their happening) or geographically (all the events in one place).

It is also possible to organize a collection of individual haiku around a title of the common element that they all share. The result of this method is called a series. Each stanza relates not to the one preceding or following it, but has a connection only to the title.

However, when you have acquired sufficient renga skills, you may begin to wish for a greater challenge. You can link your haiku, or tanka, using the techniques of the renga leaps and associations. Depending on how you form the lines and the interstitial spaces, you can find yourself doing a solo renga, or even a linked tanka—for as the three-line parts of a renga hook to the two-liners, you are basically writing a tanka. So you see that what goes around, comes around. And what you call the final resulting work is up to you.

Combining Prose and Poetry in Haibun

During the last ten years in America, more and more writers have been discovering there is increased opportunity in the technique of combining prose and poetry as revealed in Japan's oldest literary examples. Thus, what we are attempting when we write haibun, has examples in the very first recorded chronicle of the history of

Japan—*The Kojiki** One can see that already here, where history is a series of legends, there were accompanying songs or poems that were considered an integral part of the stories. Sometimes the song or poem is treated like a part in an operetta where one of the characters speaks in a less than ordinary way by singing. At other times the poem is like a summary of the story or carrier of the most important idea or feeling which is added to the end as an envoy.

We have adopted the Japanese word *haibun* (HI-BUN; *hai*, from the word haikai, with *bun* = writings, composition, or sentence), which refers to Bashō's style he used in his travel journals, for our experiments. Because he was the most famous writer who added to prose sections his hokku, we honor his work with this name for the genre. Yet he was basing his experiments on much older travel journals written in the ninth and tenth centuries, in which tanka were the poems added to the prose sections. In the imperial collections of tanka, it was sometimes necessary to include some details of the setting in which the poem was written as explanation or reason for its conception. These introductions were sometimes very short, but at other times consisted of several lines or even a short paragraph that told a little story. Though this was not seen as a style of using prose and poetry, it was, in effect, exactly that.

This device of combining some prose with haiku or

---

* *The Kojiki: Records of Ancient Matters*, written by Imperial command in the eighth century, relates the mythological creation of Japan, which until recent times was considered to be fact. A translation was first made by Basil Hall Chamberlain in 1882.

tanka solves many of the so-called problems with the brevity of haiku and tanka. The poem now acts as a torque point—where the attention is riveted on one small aspect that demands greater attention and understanding as contrast to the smooth flowing of prose.

This change of pace is so vital that one wonders why all haiku and tanka are not offered with a piece of bread called prose. One can eat slices of turkey and cheese, but how much better they taste in a sandwich. In this way haibun has its own special appeal.

So you know now how to write haiku and tanka. How do you write the prose part that goes with it to make a haibun? Some people take the easy way out and simply write down what they experienced as inspiration for the poem in a simple and direct way, which echoes the *shasei* or sketch method of writing haiku. Others feel that the prose needs to be as compacted and as linked with leaps as the poetry. Some think the prose needs to be written in a very short style—almost like an extended title—or written in a telegrammic style lacking verbs, pronouns, and sentence syntax.

The methods of almost any genre writing can be followed in the construction of the prose. The story part can form a riddle or a paradox, or display the typical tanka twist in it. At this point in our first experiments with the form, people are most often attracted to humor. In order to tell a humorous story one automatically follows the pattern of situation, with the elaboration that leads the reader's mind in a certain direction, and then inserts the punch line that reverses the previous thinking.

When telling your story, resist the desire to be too linear—instead, leap and twist. Like the mystery writer, lay down false leads and keep the reader's attention wondering where you are going with this tale.

The genre "sudden fiction" can seem to be ready-made to accompany haiku or tanka, that is if one can keep the ending open enough for the poem. If the prose "closes down" or reaches a definite conclusion, adding the poem will detract from the story's impact. The poem has to add to the prose a new dimension, to change the scene, alter the voice or time, just as the two parts of tanka relate to each other.

The way the two parts of a haibun work together determines the success of the work. The most disappointing method occurs when the story describes a situation and the poem repeats the same idea in short, while using the same nouns and the same verbs.

With a bit more skill, one can use the poem rather like an epilogue, to leap from the story to its final outcome or later result. This continues the narrative from the prose to the poem. When it wraps up the tale succinctly, it gives the reader a comfortable feeling of accomplishment and fulfills a Western literary expectation—and thus is most easy to understand. Or in the case of language poetry, it can slow down the reader's attention to the one last spin of spins of word spins spinning.

The poem part of a haibun can be used as a separate voice. As the prose piece relates an event, the poem can be used as the inside voice of the actor, or as another person's opinion involved in the incident. This is a good way of showing the dichotomy of a person's actions, and his or her thoughts. This separate voice can also be the messages of signs, as in the concept of premonitions or actual signs the protagonist reads. It is a way of telling two stories at once—which is the way life often truly is.

A refinement of this method can use parallelism. The prose part relates the two separate actions, events or persons, which are compared, associated or contrasted—just as one works with the information for a haiku or tanka.

In addition, the poem can relate to the prose by also using any of the renga or linking techniques. In this way the subject matter of the two parts may be combined to give an impression or "to say something" for which there are no words—usually a feeling or a relationship. Depending on your skills, this can be extremely subtle or fairly blatant.

Some haibun consist of a title, a prose paragraph of varying length, and the poem, and that is all. In others, additional paragraphs of prose, and/or poems are combined to make a longer work. How you do this begins to extend into theories of the book-length poem. Or the novella. Or. . . ?

Again, think of what you have learned about Japanese genres. It has been suggested that Bashō's famous *Oku no Hosomichi* (Narrow Road to the North) follows the sequential order of a renga even down to the necessity of having love lines—the night he and Sora sleep in the room next to the two prostitutes and listen to their conversations through the thin wall. Yet looking at Bashō's finished work, it is clearly chronological, so one can only say that his renga-writing expertise colored the way he recorded his journeys. The possibilities of this idea should not be overlooked.

You need not limit yourself to just haiku or tanka as the poetry form. Everything is suddenly possible, you know, and still you can be within our literary background. Even the Greek plays, written 2,600 years ago, had dialogues, monologues, and songs or chorus pieces. This idea of haibun is nothing new until you do it and make the methods fit your thinking—your vision.

Before sending your brand-new haibun off to an editor, take a few moments to check it over. Think about:

1. Does the poem really add a needed element to the piece or is it simply tacked on?
2. Does the poem repeat parts of the prose?
3. Is the prose or the poem alone sufficient for what you want to convey?
4. Knowing the difference between haiku and tanka, have you chosen the best form for your thoughts?
5. Is the prose too haiku-like, or the haiku too prose-like, or have you established an interesting contrast of writing styles?
6. Do you need more information to tell the story? Or less?
7. Is your title a working part of the technique or does it simply repeat either the prose or the poem?
8. Can you tell which of the literature construction techniques you have used?

Bashō, Japan's literary genius, spent five years rewriting and polishing the forty-two haibun in his book *Narrow Road to the North*.

The American Form of Cinquain (SIN–QUAY–N)

These short, unrhymed poems—consisting of twenty-two syllables distributed as 2-4-6-8-2, in five lines—were related to, but not copied from, the Japanese literary styles of the tanka. Though Adelaide Crapsey, an American, devised this form in the summer of 1909, in France, most of the fifteen poems she preserved were written between 1911 and 1914. An early death at thirty-seven, from tuberculosis, prevented her from exploring the genre further. This is thought to be her best cinquain:

TRIAD

These be
Three silent things:
The falling snow… the hour
Before the dawn… the mouth of one
Just dead.*

Cinquains, though they have never become very popular, have always attracted a number of poets who are still developing the form. Today, the excessive punctuation is usually eliminated in favor of a more simple presentation.

The American Form of Rengay (RAIN–GAY)

The rengay, a six-stanza collaborative form, was devised in the mid 1990s in the San Francisco Bay Area. In spite

---

* Reprinted by permission from *Complete Poems and Letters of Adelaide Crapsey* by Susan S. Smith (ed.), the State University of New York Press ©1977, State University of New York. All rights reserved.

of the associative name with renga, the rengay is intended to deliberately carry out one theme or narrative without the use of renga linking techniques. The six stanzas are unified only by the theme or title. The patterning of three and two links by two partners is exactly the same as a tan renga. This procedure is repeated two more times so that the scheme for two partners is: a - three lines, b - two lines, a - three lines, b - two lines, a - three lines, b - two lines. With three authors, the sequence is: a - three lines, b - two lines, c - three lines, a - two lines, b - three lines, c - two lines. The lines can have counted syllables as in haiku, or be flexible in short, long, short, or long, long lines, as in renga.

Sijo (SEE–JOE): The Song Form from Korea

The sijo is a Korean poetry form that first appeared in the Hyangka songs of the Sylla Empire (668–936 c.e.). It is related to the Japanese tanka by a common ancestral form of parallel quatrains from China. The sijo reached its highest point in popularity and dazzle in the sixteenth and seventeenth centuries in Korea. It is still a part of the current poetry forms, which are mostly used in songs. Actually, sijo means "song," and the name for the lyrics or poem part were called *tan-ga,* which is close enough to tanka for us to see even more connections. Remember, tanka, too have a history of being set to music—something we English speakers easily forget. Here are two fields waiting to be discovered—the various melodies for each of these poetry forms.

Around 1971, sijo started to be introduced to English

readers through articles and translations by a number of people, but their work aroused very little interest. It has been suggested that because they used free-verse translations of the originals, the fascination for the form was lost and therefore English poets failed to see any challenge in the work. It was only twenty years later, when haiku and tanka poets discovered the sijo, that they were able to use their expertise in adapting the Japanese genres to English. Thus they were able to find workable guidelines for other poets who became interested in making the sijo form their own in another language.

The sijo is defined as a three-part poem consisting of forty-four to forty-six syllables. Each part or line then contains fourteen or fifteen syllables, which is usually divided by a caesura or punctuation pause. If the sijo is printed in six lines, to make it fit narrow pages, there is usually a break in the middle of each of these lines, either as a comma or the end of a phrase. Here is an example:

> the white paint, a matted shine
> from shaved wood, eyeless terror watches
> the fanning of graceful movements
> as a woman is portrayed by a man
> who is who, one might ask
> the timeworn mask, of the Noh theater

As you can see in the above sijo, neither syllable count nor meter is as important as the melody of the phrasal quality. It is truly this that sets the sijo apart and has remained so elusive for English writers.

The sijo also stays closer to the Chinese quatrain in

following the development of the verse. The first part of a sijo sets the stage to establish the theme or the problem. The second part then elaborates, often with a parallel or matching in sense or scene. Sometimes the turn or pivot can begin here. But it is in the beginning of the third part (or line five) that the twist occurs. Then, the last of the third part (or line six) brings about a conclusion or explanation of how the parts relate.

Because the form is so new in English, there is considerable latitude in punctuation, with some authors using a minimum, others none or various mixtures of punctuation, such as the use of capital letters (to open each line? or not? sentence use?) and the spaces between the lines. However, the most important poetic aspect which defines the sijo is the musical quality and the use of the twist and resolution in the end. And there is a definite pressure from the current leaders that the syllable count remain somewhere between forty-four to forty-six English syllables to maintain the melodic aspects.

The sijo is closer to tanka than to haiku in that sijo is more lyrical and musical. It is also subjective and personal, rather than taking an objective stance as does haiku. Like both tanka and haiku, the sijo usually has a strong connection to nature and often uses parallels between nature and humanity. Like all poetry, the sijo uses metaphors, symbols, puns, allusions, and other wordplay.

Dodoitsu (DOE-DOE-ITS-SUE) for the Urban Dweller

Recently there has been some interest in a minor Japanese genre called the *dodoitsu* that has a small following among English writers. It was a traditional form for popular and folk songs and the name ("quickly city to city") appears to refer to the speed with which such new songs spread. In Japanese, the dodoitsu contains twenty-six sound units composed of four phrases in 7-7-7-5 sound units. It is hard to find examples of dodoitsu among literature because most of these songs, sung to the accompaniment of the shamisen (a banjo-like instrument with three strings), relied on the oral tradition and are therefore lost to us. Since the subject matter was either love or humor as viewed by inhabitants of the pleasure quarters, the existing works have attracted very little attention in English.

For the Epic Poet: Chōka (CHOE-KAH) or Nagauta (NAH-GA-OU-TAH, "long poem")

The chōka can be of almost any length because its form depends on alternating phrases (or lines) containing either seven or five sound units. The end of the poem is signaled by two seven units so the form is five/seven, five/seven, five/seven, five/seven. . . seven/seven. This was the most popular form of poetry in the ninth century as indicated by the large number of works in the celebrated anthology *Man'yōshū* (The Collection of Ten Thousand Leaves). This anthology of anthologies contained 260 chōka and 4,200 tanka. The poet Kakinomoto no Hitomaro, who composed most of his work in the last decade of the seventh century, took the chōka to its highest lyrical point with his finesse in the use of ritual language. The connection to tanka is evidenced by the envoy or *hanka*—a tanka-like poem attached at the end.

Occasionally more than one envoy will close the chōka. There have been a few efforts to revive the form over the intervening centuries, but the form has failed to gain any popularity in Japan, and even less has been accomplished in English.

Sedōka (SAY–DOE–KAH "repeat head poem"): A Little-Known Secret Form

This form, too, comes from the *Man'yōshū*, and is considered to be an adjacent form of the waka or tanka. The sedōka consists of six lines with the sound units arranged as five/seven/seven, five/seven/seven. As you see, the five/seven/seven form is the pattern of the lower part of the tanka which is repeated at the beginning of the poem. Sometimes this metrically identical form lends itself to the style of question-and-answer or riddle poems and was, in this way, a forerunner of renga. Yet by the time renga had developed, the sedōka was already largely forgotten. Thus the two parts of the tanka, divided now as five/seven/five and seven/seven, became the elements of the renga instead of the more evenly matched links. A few people have tried the sedōka form in English, but by ignoring the question and answer aspect of the form, they have not been able to attract a following.

Kouta (COH–OU–TA, "little song"): The Poetry of the Pleasure Quarters

The *kouta* is somewhat related to the dodoitsu, in that it also has lines of five or seven sound units and is also sung to the accompaniment of the shamisen. However, the number of lines may vary widely, and the counting of sound units varies as the songs become more ribald or jocular. There seems to be a preference for couplets of seven/five units and usually the song will end with the five-unit line instead of the preference in poetry for using the longer phrase end. The kouta grew out of the sophisticated entertainments of Old Edo (now Tokyo). Thus the songs were usually witty statements about sex, sexual behavior, and politics sung by geisha while entertaining men. Though the subject matter was often considered to be vulgar, the poems used wit, metaphor, simile, and double entendre to cloak the meanings and give new associations to love poetry. The kouta borrowed heavily from poetic techniques and often began with a statement about nature or a natural situation, before zeroing in on the topic at hand.

Kyōka (KEY-OH-KAH, "mad poem"): Really Mad Poetry

As with many Japanese literary concepts, there is a serious aspect and a comic version, and this is the nonserious side of tanka. The translation as "mad" comes across accurate but distorted so sometimes the definition of kyōka is a "comic" or ribald tanka. Actually the term is also used for perfectly serious poems which have as subjects the writing of writers writing about the form. It was not unusual for some poets to minimalize their importance by claiming only to be a writer of "mad poems." Even Bashō makes jokes about the authors of comic tanka and their poetry. In English we have not yet made a distinction between tanka on lighter subjects or tanka about tanka writing, but continue to use the same term for them all.

RESOURCES FOR FINDING EVEN
MORE ENJOYMENT IN HAIKU

Conventionally, in this part of a book, the reader just finds long lists of more books to read. Oh, I have not been lazy. I have compiled one of those lists—about forty pages long. To save a few trees, that complete list has been put on the Web (**www.ahapoetry.com/aguide**), making this work another one of the new breed of books that combines both avenues of publication.

Before you go racing away from these pages to a computer, though, I would like to give you some additional suggestions for using the lists of books, and other resources. It is too easy to get overwhelmed by mere inventories of unfamiliar names and titles, and I do not want you to end up finishing your enjoyment of haiku with this book.

First of all, if haiku and the other related forms are very new to you, I would suggest you first find an anthology of that genre. In most of them will be a review of instructions and history of the form in the introduction.

The best part is the fact that you can have an overview of what poems are being written, and by whom, so you can get acquainted with your future teachers. Here is where you can unleash your judgmental skills as you decide which works you like, and note the authors who impress you, or seem to be on your wavelength. Don't be upset if this has to be a hardcover book, because it will be one you will want to save for many years.

It is almost a given that the work and the authors you admire today will change as you grow and develop your own poetry. Keep this book handy so whenever you are feeling a bit stale, or need a new jab in your inspiration, you can come back to find another goal, and another author waiting there to help you.

Once you know whose work appeals to you, you can search for that name among the lists of individual books published by that person. By keeping this list on the Internet, it is possible for me to keep the list current as new books and authors come onto the market.

Again, if you are very new to haiku, I would first ask you to study an anthology of the genre written in English. As soon as you have grounded yourself in the form the way you wish to use it, then by all means seek out the translations of haiku written in Japanese, and other languages.

No matter how much haiku information any of us think we can pass along, there is always something new being revealed by each new translation. Do study the old Japanese masters, and the new ones, too. You will meet some very charming and interesting characters while you receive new insights into how poetry works.

Since there are at the moment no bricks and mortar haiku schools, you are responsible for your own education. This means reading books, so shove aside some old favorites, and prepare to add some new titles to your shelves.

But books are not enough. Perhaps you need to meet

the people on the other side of the printed pages. Check your local listings for poetry readings for any of the names you have seen in the anthologies or check to see if anyone is reading haiku.

Or perhaps you can find a nearby organization of persons interested in the Japanese genres that holds meetings on a regular basis. The plus about joining such an organization is that it is an excellent place to place your first poems for publication because they usually will have either a newsletter or journal or both.

Whether you can attend in person or only share in magazines depends on your location. If you can't travel to the group there are an array of online groups where you can have daily contact via user lists (a system using e-mail to send your comments and poetry to everyone who subscribes—also called e-groups) or chat rooms (where you type your statements on your computer and they instantly appear on the screens of everyone else in the "chat room" at that time). Many poetry sites have interesting interactive features to keep you entertained for months.

There are online magazines where you can submit your poems to an editor and then see them, along with those of others, on your own computer. You will find a list of them on the Web site, too.

This is not to forget paper publishing, because every year there is someone who starts a new paper-and-ink journal in these genres. A list of those is on the Web site, also. English-language haiku magazines from around the world await your perusal.

In case you run across Japanese literary terms which

need defining, the glossary that did not fit into this book can also be found on the Web site. Even if you are not looking up a certain word, I encourage you to read through it just to find things you have never thought about before. Sometimes that is all it takes to set your poetry off in a marvelous new direction.

If you are shaking your head side to side and mumbling about being a purist who does not want to even touch a computer, let me remind you that the true rustics of Japan scratched their poems on leaves with a broken twig. That ballpoint pen and commercially made note pad that keep you from having lawn litter in your file cabinet are modern inventions. If you are serious about your writing, and you must be to have gotten this far in this book, do deeply consider taking the next step in your education by getting a computer.

Yes, I know they are ugly, noisy, and far too futuristic, but that is where we are going. And wait until you discover the search engines where the world will open up before you. Join us, and visit us at **www.ahapoetry.com/aguide**.

INDEX

5-7-5   28, 52, 75

abstractions   41–42
Adelaide Crapsey   148
adjectives   37, 41, 116
adverbs   41, 73, 78
alliteration   78
allusion   120
almanac   25
Ann Cantalow   124
anthologies   51, 92
articles   32–35, 73, 76
"As Is Above: Is Below"   69
association   54, 56, 61, 64, 74, 76,
   115, 120, 134, 136
attitudes   17
awareness   17
Aware: A Haiku Primer   53

Bag of Charcoal   110
banners   100
Bashō   18, 35, 58–59, 72, 79, 98,
   110–111, 120–121, 125–126, 128–
   129, 134–135, 138, 143, 146–147,
   154
"be" form   37
beats   30
Betty Drevniok   53
binding   93, 94
body language   85
book *renga*   124
booklets   99, 103
books   92
Books in Print   95
Bowker   95
breath   30

Buson   121
butterfly   57

caesura   75
capital letters, 48, 78
CDs   87
"centering"   17
change in person   114
change in place   114
change in things   115
change in time   113
change in voice   114
childlike   68
Chime of Windbells   44
Chinese forms   107–108, 149–150
chronological order   97
chōka   152, 153
cinquain   148
close linkage   64, 133
collaborative poetry   122
comb binding   93
commas   48
commercialism   20
common language   43
comparison   53–55, 61, 64, 96, 115
computers   81, 89, 127
concepts   41
contemporary poetry   21
contrast   54, 61, 64, 76, 147, 133
copyright   89, 90
counting syllables   27, 73
"crow haiku"   59

D.T. Suzuki   66
daimyo   109
daisan   127

えいぶんはいく　たの
英文俳句を楽しむ
Writing and Enjoying Haiku

2002 年 10 月　第 1 刷発行
2010 年 9 月　第 6 刷発行

著　者　　ジェーン・ライクホールド
発行者　　廣田浩二
発行所　　講談社インターナショナル株式会社
　　　　　〒112-8652 東京都文京区音羽 1-17-14
　　　　　電話　03-3944-6493（編集部）
　　　　　　　　03-3944-6492（マーケティング部・業務部）
　　　　　ホームページ　www.kodansha-intl.com

印刷・製本所　　大日本印刷株式会社

落丁本・乱丁本は購入書店名を明記のうえ、講談社インターナショナル業務部宛
にお送りください。送料小社負担にてお取替えします。なお、この本についての
お問い合わせは、編集部宛にお願いいたします。本書の無断複写（コピー）、転載
は著作権法の例外を除き、禁じられています。

定価はカバーに表示してあります。

ISBN 978-4-7700-2886-0